PLACE CALL HOME

BY

DR. ALHASAN SISAWOI CEESAY, MD

(c) 2017 by Dr. Alhasan Sisawo Ceesay, MD

All rights reserved. No part from this book may be reproduced in any form without written permission from the publisher, except by a reviewer who may quote passages in a review to be printed in a newspaper or magazine.

FIRST PRINTING

PUBLISH KUNSA.COM

ISBN 978-1-910117-77-4

INSCRIBED TO

My Parents, Wife and Children, Teachers, Friends, Colchester Friends of Manding Charitable Trust UK and Friends of Manding Alpena, Michigan, USA; and the downtrodden

Home is a secured habitat or place one can repose, rest share with family, relatives and friends without too much of intrution from community.

Dr. Alhasan S. Ceesay, MD

PREFACE AND ACKNOWLEDGEMENTS

Home sweet home they proclaimed. So many variants exist of place we emotionally call home because of historical attachments to that place or having relocated to for better reasons. Home is abode of choice and exceptional linkage and family tires.

None of homes we are about to visit reflect opulence or riches. Nonetheless these were places that provided comfort and amicable atmosphere with security guaranteed.

It has aura or sense of security and place to repose, sleep feast and share company with family, relatives and friends. Let us ply through what these few representatives define as home.

The real names of people in this work have been avoided even if a name reminds you of a person or two who may coincidentally be identical to someone a reader knows or relates with.

The work lets us sail or follow the saga of very touching and funny tales of life, love and adventure in the home. The romantic encounters, the emotions and turbulent journeys that spark daily thrills in bosoms of our young lovers at their homes are depicted herein.

Let us then without further ado sail through sweet lips of Bintanding Nyima and Keba Kuma at their lovely home in Manka Manjang, the Gambia, in addition to many romantic stories.

Many thanks go to the numerous friends and countless supporters who encourage my writing this piece. Special thanks to my wife Mrs. Fatou Koma-Ceesay and our children: Famatanding Ceesay, Binta Ceesay and Roheyata Ceesay for persevering through thick and thin of my turbulent life in the UK and for making this work possible.

I would also like to thank readers and joint contribution of villagers whose names did not appear above. Heartfelt thanks to all of you for your kindness.

Portions of sale of the work go to help the building of the children and maternity units of the Manding Medical Centre at Njawara, the Gambia. In addition it will serve to offer scholarship to indigenous rural candidates wishing to study either medicine or agriculture and return to serve the rural sector upon completion of their studies.

Kindly browse: www.friendsofmandinggambimed.btck.co.uk or www.publishkunsa.com to learn more about our village self-help health NGO in the North Bank Region.

Dr. Alhasan Sisawo Ceesay, MD

HOW IT ALL STARTED

Once upon a time, long, long ago when there were no existing winters or sweaty summers and life was all spring like and was full of flowers, running springs, birds of unheard of beautiful plumage, an array of animals, gentle rivers to swim in or sail through and above all none scotching pleasant golden sunlight.

There existed two places called home; one where God leaved called Spiritual Dom and the other planet sphere which God used to take walks or just contemplate his next creation. These places were not known to have edifices familiar to modern day homes.

At Spiritual Dom existed God's indescribable home of the most opulent type is full of angels and stereophonic melodious voices. It is home where no hunger pains or another ache is experienced. It is place of perfection where the Almighty, king of Kings Leaves and nothing ages.

Planet Spheres on the other hand was God's architectural knack. Nothing like it has ever been replicated. It was a vast panoramic land of stunning beauty. At the time only God and his angels used it, call it for change of scenery. It was billions of years of flight wide by another trillion years of flight long.

He covered it faster than the mind can phantom. Dear friends forget the story of the great bang. There was nothing like such nonsense. Instead God decided to vary his Planet Sphere by gently slicing it into trillion upon trillion pieces each millions of miles apart and near half as big and that would make him want to put some form of different objects and creations on each.

Talk of getting busy on the job; well the Almighty had indeed set the antics higher than normal. He let these bodies fall to levels where they can accommodate his next planned creation.

Some got stock at Frigid Zones while others remained very close to burning starts we now call suns. There was one place God called Earth on which he decided to breathe life in his usual fashion. He wished for life that germinates and it happened instantaneously.

Everything had variations; above all they existed in huge numbers. In the midst of this orchestra of living things he created man. He created both Adam and Eve the same hour and day contrary to Eve being made by braking one of Adam's ribs and moulding it into a female we know as great, great Grandma Eve.

Both Adam and Eve in their angelic innocence walked separately far away to explore their newfound home. At that time neither suffered from loneliness or the pangs of romance. They mimic songs of birds or sounds of animals and basked under golden pleasant sunshine or swarm in boundless warm lakes and gentle rivers on their way.

Yes, life was very much civilized then than when blind cancerous love crept into it. One billion years later God, the Almighty, decided that it would be great to march up this pair of humans. How fast? He knew that he could replicate them to infinite numbers but that would be no fund for Adam and Eve, as their innocence would persist.

This being the case God decided that one of his angels would turn into a big, humongous but gentle snake that would wrap on an apple-like tree where Eve comes to rest.

Call it Eve's palace or home.

This snake angel would convince Eve into coaxing Adam to eat the fruit. She was told on so doing she would endure pleasure, have life doll babies after some period of nurturing them in her belly. Hundreds of years passed before Adam chanced to run across Eve.

She now under the spell of the snake-angel snubbed him and pretended smelling a lovely aromatic flower petal she plugged from a nearby plant. Adam too had been affected by the spell for the first time he started being concerned about Eve's nonchalance towards his presence.

In a worried state Adam sat on the other side of the Apple-like tree and started having strange feelings of loneliness for the first time in his life. This was something he never experienced and here he was instead of reciting his prayer verses he was fully contemplating on this feminine figure before him.

Soon the hormones in them catapulted them into an embrace they could not release. Oh no. There was no instant ala cart kissing as happened nowadays. The two just looked into each other's eyes, which spoke a million romantic verses than any poem could deliver.

Now the snake wrapped itself on the Apple tree just above Eve to allow her hear the command from it. The snake's voice said, "Beautiful one, this is your chance for the promised life doll. Hand Adam a golden ripe and juicy apple to eat and he would henceforth provide you your need in full;

so ordered the Creator; who wishes to perpetuate his creation through you." Adam too was not an easy one to rouse. He refused all approaches for fear of angering his maker. But the power of the devil surpasses man. He eventually on one very lovely evening where the blue sky was light with stars all exulting him into action. Adam accepted and tastes the apple Eve handed him. Eve plugged two succulent ripe apples from one the branches and said to Adam, "I dare you taste this fruit. It's full of sweetness found no where even in heaven." Adam took it and had a few bites and then asked that Eve finish the rest of it for goodness shakes.

It tasted good, and he ate all of it and asked for a few more apples. A short time later he had another unusual experience we now call hunger pains. From that hour to today, unlike Adam and Eve, man needed food to survive. Also right after consuming the apple the two felt at ease in holding hands, playing together in flower gardens and swimming happily in lakes.

Yes, a new heaven was opened to them even though they were unaware of the responsibility that comes with their new privilege. This went on for thousands of years until one happy Friday night they decided to push further into deep throat. A month late Eve shyly told Adam that she missed her monthly normal seeping.

Adam grew elated about the news even though he had no idea as to what was happening in Eve's body. He retorted, "Angel Eve, whatever it may be we shall rejoice at the outcome. Almighty God had a gift in mind for us and perhaps continuance."

Eve smiled and held his hands, squeezing then intermittently while looking into his eyes. Soon Eve doubled in size and her belly followed exponentially. She ate everything that came her way and nine hellish months later she delivered twins, a boy and a girl. In that day there were no christenings but the two hugged and kissed their new babies endlessly.

Adam took responsibility of gathering fruits, food and firewood to keep the clan feed, warm and happy. This new state signaled the coming of two difficult states of life. It became harbingers of aging and death. Yes, Adam and Eve will age and at the end leave the form of life they now have. The young Adams grew very fast and soon reached their teen years.

Like their parents did bygone years ago, they too decided to explore garden they were born into. The panoramic scenery of earth marveled them and they made boats and then sailed far and wide to sectors their parents never saw. This afforded them geographical advantage.

They soon decided, which is common of teenagers finding their path in this life, to settle in place they call Africum. Africum was vast and blessed with lovely sunshine, lakes, rivers, and plenty of arable land where million upon millions of different animals grace, birds of spectacular plumage and other marvels of nature existed.

Soon they too had their children, which multiplied into millions and spread to occupy more parts of Africum. Adam and Eve were delighted seeing their blood and breed prospering in God's kingdom. Soon the progenies imitated different sounds, which they adopted as their own.

This gave birth to what modern man called languages. People of same language grouped together and formed what is today's clan or tribes. For protection of the young and lovely but supposedly weak females marriage was instituted into social norms.

Today's Love

Love is embedded in all human hearts but some find their partners at magical moments of life. In this piece we will explore how that magical moment surfaced for the few-selected Madonna's and their knights on white horses who led them to the bridal lane.

Legend has it that many, many eons after the spread of progenies of Adam and Eve man's affection for another of the opposite sex became like wild bush fire spreading into all hearts and at all corners of Earth. It became ritualized and often celebrated occasion connoting maturity in some groups or tribes.

Hearts became etched into each other from mere chemistry, sight and proximity. For the love of one's country one sacrifice his or her life. Also for love of a maiden one would rather elope than follow the norms or taboos against it by society. With love came the most difficult balancing act in life.

It is enemy of over zealousness and jealousy can ruin a blooming relationship that could have turned the perfect sphere for the involved. We all remember that first electrifying moment when one endearing to us placed the first speck on our lips. How many would forget the feeling and ecstasy we then experienced.

For me it came from the blue at the age of nineteen years old. Bintanding Nyima and I had just come from the fields and as usual chatted right through the journey home never feeling the three miles distance walk to the village. Bintanding Nyima and I agreed in lot of things even though we deliberately take opposite sides at debates, like most teenagers do, in trying to impress the other.

It would take her sister's marriage ceremony for us to dare hold hands in the open. The feeling of her hand in mine sent both of us to cloud nine and never wanting to let go of each other. She looked into my eyes and smiled raising my heart rate to an unbearable peak.

Her cousin asked, "Are you two going to marry tomorrow? My dad said Bintanding loves you." This was twelve years old Fode Fatajo wondering why Bintanding and I were holding hands and with petrified eyes fixated on each other. Bintanding withdrew her grip in a sheepish manner and told Fode, "Go and play with your peers. We are just very good friends."

She then turned to me and asked, "Is it not so?" My response was uncalculated for I told Fode that he was right. Bintanding and I would one day be married, which set him running wild announcing loudly that, "Bintanding and uncle Kebba are going to marry soon." People laughed saying, "It is time they do tie the knot before Bintanding is spoken for by an interested cousin."

This statement came from those in the know and it served to worn Bintanding who was then eighteen years old. Right after Bintanding and I walked to a more quiter and discrete location. There we held hands again and debated the meaning of the advise given by the elderly women at the ceremony.

I asked, "Is it true someone wants to marry you? Do you intend to marry soon? Were they pushing the button to make us act sooner than later? I want honest answers to these very important questions." In almost tears she replied, "Rest assured that no one has yet spoken for me even though there is rumor of a cousin in Mali likely to do just that after this years' harvest.

As it stands it's just a rumor. I do not love him but my parents may not allow me waiting for an unheard of Mr. Right. I definitely would like to be married soon but it has to be to someone I love and loves me.

How about you?" she asked looking straight into my eyes with her big lovely eyes making me want to swallow her whole to prevent others ever laying their hands on her. I said "None indeed. You are the light and joy of my heart. Without you in my life I will never marry until death meets me."

It was then the most unexpected happened for me. Bintanding came close, planted her sweet lips to mine and we first kissed gently and then like wild fire relentlessly for good ten minutes before taking a breath of air. I never had such a massive high in life until then. She anchored me in heaven.

It was a sweet liquor of love and a new present in life I never experienced. It was sweet and momentous and from then on it redoubled my desire for her and my push as well as resolves to wed her in the shortest possible opportune time. The surprise arrival of the kiss and romantic impact it had on me is indescribable.

It did open the Pandora's box by unveiling and deleting fear from our hearts and letting love take over from that moment onwards. I will never love any one more than the romantic floods her presence sets in me and rises exponentially and are committed to having happiness and family we yearned.

She was beautiful to behold and to be kissed by her sweet lips was gift from the Gods. The kiss opened romantic floodgates of heaven for me. The delicious kissing was repeated several times before we decided to run home as the ceremony had ended hours ago, which will make our parents wonder where we had gone. We decided to say we went to visit Aunt Kumba Jagana who was poorly at the time. We passed by her place and auntie Jagana was very pleased and more than happy by the visit. The visit served, as an alibi should any trouble surface.

We reached home with none of us ever asked about our where about after the ceremony. It was uncle Saine who on visiting my mother told her of our good trip to see his sick sister the other day. This news pleased my parents and made them relaxed about our recently frequent disappearances and missing escapes.

Father knew about Bintanding but did not tell mother as he was waiting to have another discussion about the girl of my heart before letting it be a public domain. We will hold on for now until a couple of chapters on what followed next about this unique spark the first kiss of a lover gave me.

It cannot be replicated for sincerity and innocence accompanying it as it landed me temporally to heaven. It almost reveals why people at times get overly jealous about or to any trying to snatch their honey bunch. Love is ecstatic and blind yet very overpowering on processing and implanting its embers.

A Blind Date

Miss Bintanding Nyima was soon approached by her father and told about reasons why her Malian cousin was about to pay a visit to the family. Bintanding's heart sank to the lowest level and she wanted to die if her father insists on giving her, literally selling her, to a man she neither knew nor loved be he wealthy or as poor as a church mouse.

She decided to action while the anvil was red hot. The next day she ran away from her home and arranged that we meet at auntie's home. While there she made it clear that her family insist on handing her over to her Malian cousin due in three months time. She had made up her mind to go to Senegal to prevent her being sold to an unknown wretch.

She has decided to escape to neighboring Senegal and expects me to meet her there after six months. She told me of the pseudo name she will assume and where she would be staying in Kaulack, Republic of Senegal. We hugged amidst tears and desire for things to work out for us. Our love for each deserves something much better than this Alice in wonderland fairy tale or current darkness about to beset us.

Sure enough time was too slow for me. I could not bear missing her six long and lonely months without seeing her. It meant eons of solitude for me. I even feared her falling in love with a Senegalese or getting into an unbearable difficulty while on her self-exile from her parents. The six months were needed strategy to avoid the sudden disappearance of Bintanding being linked to my family or I after their approach, in my behalf for me to marry Bintanding was rejected outright by Bintanding's parents. At Kaulac she became known as Musu Foro, meaning the honest lady. She was lucky to get a lucrative and well paying job at one of the supermarkets in the city. I was put on surveillance by all her relatives and their friends and even the police got involved but had to stop harassing me because there was no justification to substantiated allegations that I had a hand on the sudden disappearance of Bintanding Nyima.

The police at Kaulac did sent report to their Gambian counterpart on reports of sightings of a lady with similar description but on checking it was found that the said lady was a born Senegalese who the mayor of Kaulac attested to knowing and having been to her christening some twenty-one odd years ago.

Having now settled and her parents believing not to ever see their daughter alive gave up searching for Bintanding and exonerated my family and me. They literally became our best friends. It would be seven months before I made my move.

It came during a wedding ceremony of a distant family member who leaves in Senegal though at Mburr village some fifty miles away from Kaulac where Bintanding Nyima alias Muso Foro was staying free. While there I joined the fellows to go buy some soft drinks and have chance to see Kaulac and accidentally we ended up going to the supermarket were Bintanding works.

I never knew that she was an employee at Sedal hol supermarket. My friends saw her and decided to coax her to meet me after working. She was told who the Gambian was but her identity was kept away from me for fear of my collapsing or blowing up her cover as a pseudo Senegalese.

It would be 8:45 pm when Bintanding Nyima, now Musu Foro, appeared being even more beautiful than I had imagine. She leaped toward me with hands stretched and arms wide open. She said "Darling, I knew you would not abandonee me to the wolves.

Your friends told me about your visit and it was no accident that they brought you to the supermarket. Thank God you are well and still looked handsome as ever." We hugged and kissed several times before I could get out my dumb foundedness. It was pleasing to hear and feel her heart pounding by mine.

We spent most of that evening at Mballah show given by Yusu Ndure and company. The night went fast as we up date each other and made plans on the next step to cement our relationship. Our options were as indicated bellow.

1. We could marry in Senegal for she was now a Senegalese by virtue of all documents at the police.
2. Give her parents chance to reunite with her on the understanding of making them to accept her love for me.
3. Marry and elope to France and never to return home for almost fifteen years. We finally agreed on allowing her parents realize her choice in whom she marries which will give many blessings to our wish to unite for good and it would keep current warm friendship between our parents better appreciated.

This blind date rejuvenated us and we thanked my friends for job well done. However I had to leave the next day but would have her parents know she is alive and well and having a good job. Mean while my Malian competitor had given up and married to another girl not far away from Bintanding Nyima's village.

Her parents kissed my hand and apologized for not only refusing me marry to one that percolates my heart but also for the attitude and way my delegation was thrown or rebuffed. Her father said, "Son, the ball game is now at your court.

If you send for her hand in marriage we would gladly acquiesce and no one will over ride my decision to give my only daughter to one that kept her alive through the past nightmare." He prayed for our happy union in due course and assured me that they back Bintanding's father who would stand by his words to being an amiable father in law.

Dr. Alhasan Ceesay resting after hours of book writing

Alas! The Bridal Lane

Marriage was something of a preoccupation in our minds. We spoke about it nearly ten times in most days and finally the waiting was almost over. Bintanding returned for good to the Gambia from the Republic Senegal where she took refuge for the past three and half years.

She went to Senegal to avoid being forcibly married to her Malian cousin who by tradition would have own her and she to obey his wishes and commands be they reasonable or not. She refused to be anyone's beautiful maiden slave whose only purpose in life is to satisfy the husbands' libido while cooking and caring for his children.

Bintanding and her peers no longer stoop for such exploitation by men. These men were normally useless ones too. The community welcomed her return and everyone assured her their desire to see her wed the man of her heart and choice. Just amidst this jubilations another rich cousin from Guinea Conakry threw wrench into the fray by throwing his hat into the field ready to pay ten times amount Keba Kuma was able.

In addition he promised to provide Bintanding Nyima life of a "Rose Garden" abided with servants to her mercy. All she had to say was yes and the village would turn into Eden's garden. Bintanding's father got angry with the greedy brothers of his for encouraging this rich brat to upset happiness of his daughter.

He called all elders and both Bintanding and I and made it crystal clear that no one was going to disturb our plans and he would personally kill any that interferes with his decision to have us marry. We left the room very happy having guarantee from both parents.

The next day saw the arrival of Bintanding's rich cousin from Guinea Conakry on a white Arabian horse followed by a dozen servants carrying loads of gold and many other heavenly or princely presents.

Bintanding and I decided to take a walk to her auntie, another supporter of our cause, some thirty miles away to leave the fool display his wares, which he believed would purchase Bintanding's love and heart. We were not going to have him have the pleasure of setting eyes on Bintanding or test my determination to ward off any suitor.

We later learnt that the village sent him and servants running for life the moment Bintanding's parent told them not to step by their gate as they have no wife to offer him." He was said to have said, "My daughter was better than your gold or gilders and we do not care remaining poor as long as we die knowing we made her happy by letting her wed the man she loves and not one that purchased her."

Greedy friends of his blamed him for being a compound fool by rejecting a rich man in favor of one who could hardly feed himself. He was said to have told such friends to ride with the rich cousin to hell and that they were no longer his friends for money has no master. He wanted his daughter marry one that loved and respected his daughter not some show off.

Finally, all neighboring villages pitched in adding whatever money and goods they had towards the dowry. In the end the Nyima family received far more than they would have had they acquiesced to greed and accepted offer from the rich cousin from Guinea Conakry. Alas! All is now set for the wedding day.

The grand Imam sanctified our marriage two Fridays before the real ceremony. Bintanding had lots of dresses made for her plus embroidery one that I personally got for her. Off course she choused to wear the one I bought for her instead of the special embroidery ones the community gave her to mark the occasion.

Two months later suitors were now certain of never ever getting to be husband to my Bintanding. The wedding ceremony started early Saturday morning spilling over to the wee hours of Sunday. There was singing and dancing that even angels swayed with rhythm coming from the drums.

Yes, the bride was ravishingly charming in her traditional embroidery bridal dress, which she proudly wore in honor of her love for me and to mark the one-day she would never repeat again for the rest of her life.

Unlike most we spent our honeymoon at our new home at the outskirt of the village. People from far and near poured in expressing happiness and extending their helping hands of all types. We welcomed our first born ten moths later and that christening was one of a kind in the history of the region.

Our looser the rich cousin from Guinea came and pretended to host the affair but again was rebuffed by villagers and the police. That was the last we heard from or about him and his lonely wealth.

Mrs. Famatanding Tarawaleh, Mother

What Will I do Without Your Kiss?

Love and its endless stories commits us follow the romantic saga of two blind lovebirds. What makes one who does not see or differentiate another to become so chemically attracted to each other? In the normal world, sight, voice and character has a lot to offer in creating relationship.
The only sight a blind person has is feeling, by touching things or hearing voices but this is by no means a gage for aesthetic value.
To answer these and many more wonders of human nature lets turn to story about Wude Nyabali and Kemo Finkinte. Neither Wude nor Kemo ever had glimpse of the sun or their environment. They were born blind like a bat from day one of their lives. There are no guard dogs in Africa and hence the blind relies wholly and solely on sound, and feeling.
One almost risk saying or asking how do they keep a mental map of the places in their heads but then how do we map things that we do not see physically? Any how it was on a bright Saturday morning when Wude Nyabali was heading to the Loomo, a local market day when one can buy things at almost give away prices, when out of the blue she heard a melodious singing voice or what sounded like music from an angel coming from her left side.
Wude decided out of curiosity to follow the sound's source. She too sang the same song causing the other to ask, "Who is that sweet voice stealing my poem?" At this juncture Wude was a stone throw away from Kemo Finkinte. A silence followed before Kemo started reciting his poem again. Only this time a hand was feeling him as to map his shape.

He retorted and asked, "Who dare frisk me?" A very amiable voice responded, "It is one your luring melodious voice drew to you and want to have feel of such a good person reciting love poems and songs so touchingly." Kemo Finkinte could not believe the romantic magnetism in the voice he just heard.

He said, "My name is Kemo Finkinte and I was born blind. And who are you? Are you one of those who love to tease me? Tell me your name and I will instantly reward and sing you your own special poem right now." Wude Nyabali's heart rose while her head disbelieved what she heard. "My own love poem did you say?

I am Wude Nyabali and have been equally like you born blind since birth. I have never experience romantic love. How can you sing or make one genuine poem for me?" After this Kemo turned and started to feel her and sort of have a mental map of her. He then told her that, "You are the most gorgeous feminine I ever felt.

The touch of you left my heart fluttering endlessly for want of you. Will you promise never to be away from my side? And together we will explore that romantic world, which has eluded both of us because of defect we never choused in life nor do we wish any to have.

Your tantalizing voice has become added sight and gift from the Almighty God for us. I feel being in heaven with you standing by me." Wude Nyabali in tears replied, "The same applies to me. Hearing you was good luck but touching you was more than heavenly for me too. I will wait here until you finish your recitals and together we will go to the Loomo.

I have a place I stand where good people give me money and things to eat or use. You and I can team up from henceforth." At first Kemo's stubborn male pride or call it instincts made him want to refuse the offer of partnership but then love has its necklace round his neck a hundred times and his heart has fallen weak for this equally blind dame requesting a welcomed and deserved favor from him.

Mr. Sisawo Ceesay, Father

Dr. Ceesay and wife Fatou Koma-Ceesay

Dudou Ceesay, Brother in green with family

Mrs. Binta Ceesay, Sister

Mrs. Famatanding Tarawaleh, mother

Alasan Mballow, Jr with Auntie Roheyata Ceesay, 2014

Mrs. Fatou Koma-Ceesay

Mrs. Fatou Koma Ceesay, Oldham, UK 2017

Miss Famatanding Ceesay, Daughter

Miss Binta Ceesay, Daughter

Miss Roheyata Ceesay, DFaughter

Dr. Alhasan Ceesay graduating from the American Univ. of the Caribbean School of Medicine, Plymoth, Monsderrat West Indies 1992

Dr. Alhasan S. Ceesay holding Africa

He told her, "Okay, only if we do not have fights over which directions to take." Wude replied, "Darling rest assured the only ones we will have from now on would be romantic pillow fights but not temperamental or physical fights." The two blind lovers walked towards the loomo holding hands while Kemo Finkinte lead the way. At the Loomo and in place where Wude Nyabali stations there were lot of people waiting for her and who started getting worried that she did not turn up.

It was unusual not to find her seated and begging for alms at this spot on a loomo day. Only this time, applause and relief from those concerned about her welfare greeted her arrival. They too saw the magical link between her and Kemo even though neither Wude nor Kemo volunteered to say anything about the duo. It would take a seven-year-old girl called Nyimanding to spill the beans or pry the truth out of Wude Nyabali and Kemo Finkinte.

Nyimading said, "I definitely know you two are in love for the way you smile at each other reminded me of how my brother used to smile at his now wife when they meet. Am I right you are lovers? All of us here will celebrate with you should you tell the truth now."

The child's query drew more and more people closer to the blind stars of the day and in dead silence awaiting a reply from either Wude Nyabali or Kemo finkinte. It was Kemo, who to the delight and surprise of all spectators at the Loomo, who knelt holding Wude Nayabalis' hand and asked, "Wude will you be my loving wife.

I will be the luckiest blind person to be wedded by you. As blind people we will work our way through life and together we can forge a lot of good. I love you Wude Nyabali and please allow me marry you coming Friday by God's will."

Wude Nyabali in tears said, "This is the greatest dream any woman wished fulfilled.

I loved you the moment I heard you reading those poems and more so when I felt you. I knew you are mine. And yes, I am your wife for the rest of our lives and will take care of both you and our children should we be endowed with any. I will tell my family about this good news and about endearing love we have for each other."

Wude instantly hugged Kemo and they kissed unabashed at the loomo. People were moved and they all in unison said we will see to it that your forthcoming wedding ceremony be the most memorable and historic than any ever witnessed at Njawara.

They hugged and congratulated them over and over. Then it was Nyimanding, the seven-year girl's turn to hug them saying, "I am very pleased for you two. God make your union the most cherished in the region. My mum and I will do all we can to tell our villages join others in making your day memorable not only for you but for the whole region. Thank you for proving me right in my intuition about you. I am happy for you."

This said everyone at the Loomo donated money or food to mark the wedding due to take place Friday coming.Mean while the two were given loads of money, rice, and fruits to take home. One of the farmers helped them take the things in his cart and helped them store it safe at Kemo Finkinte's house.

Wude Nyabali went to be with her family not far away and happily shared the good news of the day with everyone.Both sighted and none sighted pitched in to make union of Wude Nyabali and Kemo Finkinte the best in the Badibous.

Their wedding would coincide with the farmers' thanks giving after harvest known as "Mmansa Bengo." It meant more people will witness marriage of the people's favorite none sighted couple.

On the day of the wedding Wude Nyabali was given dressing make up by the best of the best in the region leaving her look more radiant any ever envisaged. She was rendered stunningly beautiful but sadly her husband would never see it but believe it from comments attendants and friends were offering. There was drumming, dancing and singing all through the day and scribes recorded it as the greatest blind wedding ever held in the Badibous.

The village gave them land and built a home where the couple stayed there after in happy marriage and raised all six children of four brilliant boys and two beautiful girls. Interestingly none of their children was born blind. They went to school and today the two girls are both pediatricians while two of their brothers became high power lawyers and of the last two, one became a professor in mathematics while the other a business tycoon. Kemo Finkinte was once in replying to the question, "Do you see being blind as a handicap? Kemo confidently emphatically said, "No! Being born blind is no handicap for I can do most of what you the sighted can only that I do not see women like you do." People laughed. He continued, "However let me tell one and all I will make her the happiest wife on earth." This he fulfilled in his marriage to Wude Nyabali as they became the envied of all around and they even help set up Badious blind association catering to needs of the blind and their children. Wude Nyabali Finkinte in replying to the same question said, "My children proved how normal we are.

Only an aspect of ours' is missing compared to you. We have feelings and needs like you and above all we always yearn to reach out and touch others. This desire made a poet out of Kemo Finkinte and a good singer dancer out of me. We are grateful to all of you for making life much desirable." This story leaves us saying all is well that ends well.

L – R: Dr. Alhasan Ceesay, Prof. Sulayman Nyang and Professor Francis Conti, Atlanta, Georgia 1985

Is There Real Justice to Love?

It is said that, "There is no respite for the wicked." Love has many tentacles to grasp and twist our fate. Each of the above couple had two unknowns they took resort to when they were separated and divorced.

The truth and question is that would these hidden individual stay clear off the blessings that surfaced for our ladies and their gentlemen? Dr. Fondike's unknown called and gave the following black mail threat from an Italian sounding voice the Dr. almost recognizes, "Listen supper doctor.

I will tell the media crap you were involved with if you fail to drop $20, 000 into my account by noon Monday. You get it? Take a look at your door an enveloped has just been dropped for your eyes only. It contains photos of you shagging your secretary. Get going and deliver the goods now.

You do not want madam to have to learn about it from the news media. Do You?" The caller rang off instantly to avoid being traced. The great doctor rushed to the door to get the envelope before his Barrister wife walks in. He opened it hurriedly and found two undesirable photos of him in action with his former secretary.

His first reaction was asking why the secretary blackmailed him in such a dishonest way. The second was to tell his wife the moment she walks in. Or just pay the ransom money and keep everything under the carpet. Let us see what love will do in this intriguing case. He thought about it amidst tears and fears of more calls asking for even higher amounts.

After two hours of brainstorming he concluded that he would come out clean to his wife and would involve the police and Interpol as the call originated from Italy. He was worried to death about telling his wife but tell he most because he does not want to loose her any more especial because of his past behaviours.

He called Kering Marena, one of his trusted confidants and put the case before him and seeked advice for sensible approach especially with the wife whom he does not want to loose.

Kudang Kering rang later and said, "I thought through about the hairy state you are in but if it were me I would call good friends and in theirs' and your wife's presence spill out all the beans and dirty laundry of your life prior to the marriage, especially during the first one.

She would be dismayed and angry at first but love will make her accept that you at least brought it in the open instead of paying the ransom and hiding it from her. Failure to take corrective measures will subject you to constant black mail and media ridiculing."

Dr. Fondinke in response acknowledged the points raised and promised to do as suggested right away. Hence, when Barrister Yama walked into her sitting room she was shocked to see worried faces staring at her. At first she thought whether her father-in-law had not passed away because of the serious look in her husband's face.

She put her bag and greeted the visitors and right then and there asked her husband what was the matter that brought these friends with such sad mood on their fancies. He said, "Honey it's very bad and is in regard to something that I need discussed with you but the atmosphere at Bridgeport made it slipped my mind.

I am very sorry but I called these honest elderly ladies and gentles to witness my telling all in the clearest and most honest manner." The preamble was too long for Yama and so she broke in and asked, "Honey will you come to the point because it has been a long day at court.

There is nothing we cannot solve alone in the privacy of our home. But you see it fit to call these fine people to mediate. That is well and fine with me as long as justice is maintained. Fire on we are dying to hear your epic story of the year"

The doctor took a deep breath and said, "Hear it. Hear me thus. Back during and when we were divorced I used to have some temptation and affairs with my secretary. It was because of that I agreed to foot her education bill in the USA on the promise that she will never tell or surface near me any more.

Four hours ago I received an international call from Italy demanding a ransom of $20,000 by noon Monday or my name will become fodder for the newspapers. Upon serious thought of our new commitment to each other I chorused to reveal all my then dirty laundry before you and these honest people and at the same time beg for your forgiveness in the past and now."

Yama in shocked and almost puking, said, "Give me time to think while I change into something light." While alone up stairs she asked, "Why I lord? I loved this man. Why are they still after him?" Barrister Yama Chorr can talk out of any situation except when it concerns Dr. Ke Fondike, a gorgeous consultant with smoldering eyes and lean body that does not quit making every movement promising sophisticated sex.

She asked, "What woman would not go tongue tired or fight to retain him? It would certainly take some super spirited encounter to separate me from my man." Then all of a sudden she remembered having similar arrangements with a trainee doctor of her husband. She told herself, "Two wrongs do not make a right.

Both of us had our misbehaviours. I will stand by my husband and fight tooth and nail against these extorting bandits." She washed her face with cold water and then braced to tell her own side before and after their divorce. She even believes that the call to emanate from that silly doctor who has family in Italy.

She sat down with misty eyes and said, "Honey, I too have dirty laundry to confess to. Remember your trainee Italian doctor, Alexandro? He and I had something going during and after the marriage. He proposed and I rejected him on the grounds that you were the only man I fully ever loved.

So I am not surprised at the call coming from Italy. Was it with a Spanish or Italian drooling Spanish accent? I am very sorry and I give you my wholehearted commitment to standby you and whatever the threat do not give into paying money we need for future of our children. Let the bandits work for their living instead of believing on extorting people to the last drop of blood."

He handed her the envelope and she screamed, "That beach! I will kill her any time I find her a hundred miles near you." She definitely did not appreciate seeing her husband and another woman in such a compromising position. It was unacceptable. She bellowed out loud, "I hope we learnt our lesson and that such things would never happy again. Are you sure you will not surprise me with other hidden unknowns? I have told you all about my escapes and that was the only person who got to know me. Again am very, very sorry but had aired it out to maintain the new thrust we have in each other." Alas, both saw the light at the end of the tunnel. They jointly went to the police and told them more than were said before their friends.

The police linked with Interpol and soon Dr. Alexandro was arrested and brought to court in Italy. What happen to Binta and Musa's closet friends? This time it was the lady in question Marie Jaiteh Mokapoch. Marie refused marrying any suitor that asked for her hand in marriage. She vowed to die a sphincter if she fails to be wedded by tycoon Musa Koditi.

Musa is fitly rich fellow of the region. Musa did have brief encounters with Marie Mokapoch and had even smuggled her to France in one of his trade missions. Marie had the servant make duplicate keys of the Manson Musa lived and deliberately sneaked in one evening just in time to allow Binta Rafet to find her sprawled in her master bed.

A chamber only Binta Rafet and her husband or the cleaners were allowed. Binta screamed out of shock and surprise before gathering her breath or self and asked, "What da f, f, and mother f, are you doing in my chambers?

Who the mother fff are you? Tell me before I call the police to take you to the lunatic home." Marie nonchalantly got up, looked at her face in the mirror, worked very close to Binta Rafet and whispered in her ears, "I was there before and after you and shall be the one that removes you from this comfort.

Do you understand little girl?"At that provocation Binta gave her a good but very heavy slap on the face sending Marie to flat on the floor. She lay unconscious until the arrival of an ambulance with a medical team. Marie Mokapoch was resuscitated and taken to hospital for observation and overnight stay.

The police and Musa Koditi were summoned to the Manson to look into the detail of the crime and why it happened. Binta Rafet turned into a volcano the moment her husband stepped in. He managed to take her to one of the private rooms and spilled out the beans about all his relation with Marie Mokapoch and how he tried to keep her away but to no avail.

Marie, upon recovering told police how she paid to have a copy of the keys made for her and how she knew the time that both wife and husband would be away to enable her ease into the Manson un-noticed. She apologized and confesses that love for Musa Koditi drove her into all the past and current crazy acts.

She asked to be escorted back to Musa' Manson to apologies to Binta Rafet and to plead with Musa to keep Binta Rafet as wife. She promised not to ever disturb their marriage.Was Binta in the mood to forgive or receive an impostor? We shall soon know. Binta was initially charged with assault with intent to cause malicious bodily harm to Marie pending the finding of the police investigative team at the hospital.

To her surprise she saw Marie Mokapoch brought under police escort to the house. As soon as the sergeant entered Marie pleaded to be heard. She started by way of an apology and then said, "Through my teenage days to today Musa Koditi was the only one I ever fancied.

Things got a little serious at one time when he contemplated on sending Kola nuts to my parents to ask for my hand in marriage. It never materialized because of some ancient tribal bickering between the two families. Then he married you Binta Rafet. Who by all means was self made as we all noticed in her wealth and worldwide assets.

Blinded by love I lost my senses in hope of the flimsiest chance of dethroning her and getting my man. Until yesterday I never knew how much Binta Rafet loved this man until after she land that thunder of slap which sent me to sleep for quite a while.

I am still afraid of being near her or any one that looks like her. She is a kind lady and I cannot pick spilled water but would she, woman to woman, please forgive me? I promise not to ever come near or speak to her husband. I have now willingly surrendered him to her to keep forever.

May their marriage bloom in good health." Every one present felt sadden and moved by her candor. Musa Koditi also apologized for forgetting to bring this dark part of his life before his wife. It was Binta Rafet who said, "Marie, I admire you for I am a woman and would have possibly done the same or more to keep the love of my heart.

I am sorry you had to go through all this pain and trouble of sneaking into my chambers. As far as I am concerned you are completely forgiven on condition that you keep away from my darling for good.

You are young and I am certain there is a Mr. Right knight out there ready to gallop with you to the bridal lane of connubial life. Men can be challenging for us but we all make mistakes because we are not angels.

Again, you are forgiven but be warned to keep clear of our fence for the rest of your earthly life." Marie Jaiteh Mokapoch thanked Binta and begged the police to drop all charges against Binta Rafet with regards to intruding into the compound. All concord and the charges were dropped with everyone going home peacefully and happy. This bright end did not prevent the media to harp on it for two publications.

They titled most of their articles about the case under the heading "The injustice of love." As it already surfaced it looked like Binta Rafet was the only one free of a dirty laundry and this brought as well as earned her more respect and love within the community.

The couples became new paramour soul mates bearing many children in the years following their reunion. Many citizens named their first girl child after Binta Rafet hoping the children will turn As rich and as honest as Binta Rafet of Njawara village, Lower Badibou, The Gambia,

West African dark caves and doomed dungeons. In life we must extend our hearts to others and with compassion reach the needy of our communities. Careers of the aged, the sickly and disable deserve mention in being among the greatest golden hearts of our time. Bravo.

Mrs. Famatanding Ceesay-Maballow, Daughter

ODES TO TENDER LOVING CARE

This Ode is dedicated to those who tirelessly gave themselves for the love of the other. A hungry peasant in the street given a piece of bread, a penny or a shilling makes his day and only caring love made the giver act in kind.

Yes, the little acts of kindness we show are lives saving and it helps to give hope to others, especially the despondent and down trodden. Ignorance can at times be callous as demonstrated in the treatment of lepers in the olden days.

Today a bit of TLC and medication allowed these to leave among society instead of spending the rest of their earthly life in to all those gallant men and women who go to help in disaster zones, earth quakes, fire, or Tsunamis catastrophes. They do this out of love for you and me at the risk of their own very lives.

I applaud wholeheartedly farmers who keep our breadbaskets filled, sailors who brave turbulent stormy oceans to get commerce moving, firemen who challenge fires and fishermen who face angry seas to land a catch in other to provide us delicious fish meals,

Teachers who impart knowledge in us and all those bright minds that fly the metal birds to make global trotting lot easier than Christopher Colombo's days. There is no greater TLC than it. Those with Alzheimer suffers can for sure attest to the dedication, patients, and love these unique people show as being fact of pure love for the self and others.

No one can pay enough for the services of the housewife with husband and ten kids running around, Nurses, doctors, teachers, careers, police and even the solder. What they give to society keeps all safe and informed for the day. They give safe TLC to allow us have restful nights like babies in slumber land and wake up to more TLC.

Even young women can at times be overheard telling their friends that they intend to give tender loving care to their men when the men return from work. Yes, everyone needs and love TLC ala cart. Do not we feel great in the loving arms of our wives or lovers or mums? One should be thankful when someone else cares about us.

Note the love and care a mother gives to her newly born. Nothing is greater TLC than maternal love and the eventual bonding that ensues between mother and child. Love makes us forgive and forget pain inflicted on us. Without TLC the world will be in endless storms.

TLC is a charitable act that pervades all spheres of communities. TLC makes our hearts etched in others forever. TLC gives inspiration to the despondent and down trodden and it raises our spirits to higher heights. Hurray To TLC!

Cheers go to my wife and friends for loving me and for caring for both of us in this life. Tender loving care is phenomenon found in all higher mammals. Just watch documentaries about our cousins' monkeys, Apes, Gorillas, and Chimps and one would certainly note tender loving care being endlessly dispensed. In the ghetto Tender Loving Care implies giving heart, soul, and feeling to the self and others.

TLC magically transience gender and age. The old lady or man afraid of crossing the street would tell you relief he or she had from the gentle touch of a Scout or a police officer volunteering to help them cross to the other end of the street. It was all TLC in action and it leaves gratifying feeling for both giver and receiver.

"Always be my TLC." A true friend once sent this wish to me on my 50th birthday being a valentine day while I was in America. Hence we valentines do receive lot of cheers and TLC on our revered February 14th day of our lives.

It is normally said that business neither has a heart nor does it bleed but take it from me it does give TLC to its shareholders and governments that can dole millions if not billions of taxpayer's money to bail them for eating or spending in unsafe investments our invested monies within their worldwide network of banks.

TLC is strong feeling almost mystical in itself. I wish governments had the same heart or TLC to bail out ordinary folks like you and I from grips of unyielding joblessness, poverty and disease. Aids, Malaria, AK47dictocrats of the developing world, and rampant corruption are drowning mankind. Where has the governments' TLC for man gone?

We asked. TLC, TLC! My brothers and sisters bind us for good. At times I hear people moaning about the emptiness of life and turbulent waters it landed them. The urge to tell or ask if they ever tried the not so much of panacea TLC for it could just be the bridge they needed to get them over trouble waters of their lives. Tender loving care to you and may TLC forever remain etched in our hearts. TLC is bounty wider than the Atlantic and deeper than any earthly ocean. The more we give ourselves to help others the more we receive from it. Like my valentine card, back in my student days in America yearned, I too ask readers to always give tender loving care to themselves and others. Cheers.

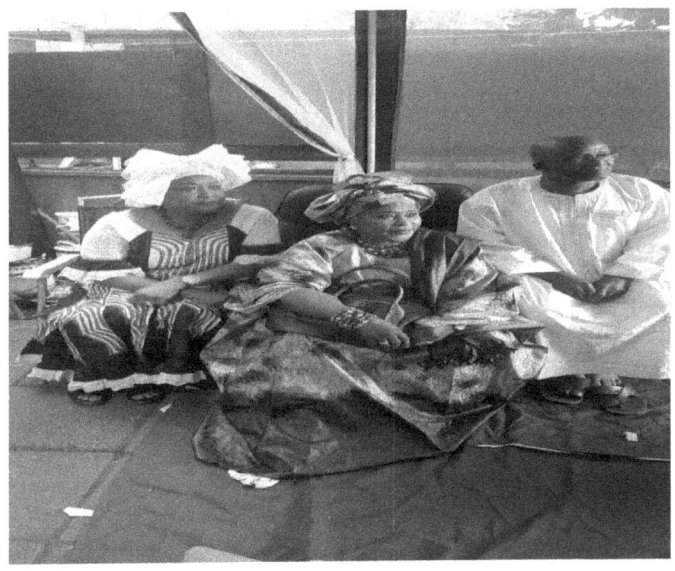

L-R: Sukai Bouvier Sali Darbo Kebba Dampha

Delicious Love Encounter

One never in reality taste love but in the case of the couple we are about to meet. It tasted sweeter than honey and the best thing that ever happened in their lives. Long time ago, in 1934, Bajoja Ceesay on a trip to Njawara from Njaba Kunda village ran across pretty Miss Salla Hanti Sey on her way to fetch water from a nearby well.

Bajoja lost both his heart and head upon sighting this beautiful Fulani girl. He upon arriving at Panne Ba village asked who the parents of girl were. Pate Fula the uncle of the girl in question was nearby happened to hear Bajoja's enquiries and came to find out what might have happened to his nice.

After a friendly handshake and greetings, Bajoja told Pate, "I have never come across a female with such beauty and perfection in my life." Pate's response shook Bajoja. Pate told him, "We are Fulas and will never cast our children to tribe you came from. It will indeed be a great loss as she would never tend cows or milk them.

We are Shepherds and wish to remain so." Bajoja could not stop himself from retorting, "Friend, there is much to life than tending and milking cows, sheep or goats. There is that ethereal thing that is called love and it is blind. Love has no boundary; nor does it obey any tribal rituals. It's a mover of mountains that legions are unable to tackle. It owns the heart and hence remains restless until it achieves its goal.

Its end is left to no one but those concerned whose hearts it glued tightly than any your cow will provide." The two left without a word. But Pate was not going to have it end at that. He called a family meeting and told them all Bajoja said short of saying he was prosing to marry his nice. The family was equally worried that their daughter was getting astray.

Hence, innocent Salla Hanti Sey was summoned to an emergency meeting with the family elders, including her dad, mum and aunts. Poor thing was shocked because the stranger in question never said a word to her nor did they ever meet at any time in her life.

She wondered why the hyped and concern about an innocent man just passing through to Njawara. As soon as she stepped forward, her father Musa Bah said, "You are summoned by our elders because something of great concern to us about you have reached our ears. All we want is the truth and nothing but the truth of what transpired between you and that Bajoja Ceesay who had the galls to ask about you and your parents.

Of what interest do you have in him? We are Fulas and do not want our children burring their heads in sad like Ostriches in the desert." Undoubtedly every thing came from the blue for poor Salla and after brief moment she started believing that some of the drinks left these men soak in water and it may have gone into their heads to make them think or dream of things that never happened.

Her long silence made her mother Hanti Bah to cry and begged her to tell the truth. Salla Hanti Sey finally woke up from her stupor and said, "Mum, dad and elders, all I say here is nothing but the truth and I give you my word to scarify me if it turned otherwise.

First, I never met, nor have I spoken to the said Bajoja Ceesay. He did passed some fifty yards away from the well that Kumba Bah, Grandma Gaye, and Hadi Pane were drawing water from the well. He never even greeted us.That was the first sighting of him and I am very surprised that uncle Pate saw it fit to make such fuss or ado about nothing.

Perhaps he might shed light right here and now as to what led him to convene such baseless meeting that tarnishes my name and that of my dear mother. I challenge all to question the above named if there was an iota of lies in what I just told.

This was what transpired and the truth about said gentleman Bajoja; I mean what did you say was his sure name? I rest my case in the hands of Almighty and merciful God."

All turned around and looked at Pate Bah because candor and braveness of Salla Hanti Sey tend to point to the other direction and now fingers turn to Pate who was asked to repeat what he told his brother Musa Sey in private after the afternoon prayer.

Pate Bah stood with his legs almost giving up. He was shaking and the elders had no time for pity. They wanted the truth to avoid shedding blood of the innocent. Pate knows that he could be at the least ostracized or burnished if found guilty and smearing innocent Salla Hanti Sey.

He started by saying that he met the said gentleman while the man was enquiring about parents of Salla Being her loving and concern uncle he stepped up and asked why Bajoja Ceesay was enquiring about the girl. He even told the elders that he asked if something sinister happened but thank God the man just told him about love and how blind and that it had no boundary. He continued and said, "I assumed him, meaning Bajoja Ceesay, to be one of those bad men that elope with our girls. "It was such parental concern that made me meet my brother Musa and asked that we cut the bud before it blooms into branches and our losing our lovely daughter.

One need not ask grandma, Hadi or the other lady because I found out from them that the man indeed never said a word to any of them. He just passed and continued towards Njawara village. I had already spoken to Musa and was about to reveal my finding to him when I found you assembled to interrogate Salla Hanti Sey.

She stands innocent and had spoken the truth. The whole thing was a baseless assumption in my part. I am sorry. Please accept my apologies to all of you for being kind to me, especially to Grandma, Salla Hanti and her parents. I am very sorry and would abide by any decision or punishment you levee on me for being so stupid not to check things out thoroughly before become a scaremonger.

Again accept my apologies." By the time old man Pate finished tears were running down many cheeks. The old man had never made such mistake in seventy years of his life. The grandfatherly concern overpowered him to assume something cynical was about to rear its head and it needed to be dealt with before it blooms.

After a lengthy deliberation, Salla Hanti was called and asked if she would ever forgive her uncle and if she would go along any decision made by them. Salla looked into the eyes of Pate and said, "If I were to have an uncle it had to be him. It was out of great fear and concern for my welfare that led my dearest uncle into the pit.

I have forgiven him with all my heart and I now love and respect him more than ever. I promise to name my first boy child after him. No one is perfect in more than seventy years this is the only black speck in his wonderful life of caring. I now plead for mercy and for us to celebrate a good man but he is no traitor to my name or me. May the merciful God guide you in your final deliberations."

People were moved by her wisdom, maturity and kindness in being forgiving that they each hugged her and thanked her for making a very difficult job easier. Old man Pate Bah was by now in tears and suffered a trance. All said and done the case was closed with no penalty levied upon Pate. The next day Pate was in good health to hear the verdict. He promised to stand by his nice for the rest of his earthly life.

Beautiful Binta Ceesay

Never Let Me Go Away

It is said that thunder ball or bolt never strike at the same spot twice but in saga we are about to unfold it did that with precision. Legend has it that Mrs. Mary Lovenut had in her early years had a crush on a Blackman but was afraid of being lynched if discovered by society she grew from. Well it is said that what goes round comes round and back.

Her short encounter with Kunsa's uncle ignites her youthful feelings and she and Kebba discovered something very magnetic and unusually strong between them. However, they managed to meet secretly at a friend's house and boy; oh boy did he give it to her.

She told him at the end of vigorous enjoyable sexual encounter, "No wonder my daughter would sell me to retain your nephew. African men are hot and perfect delicious delicates." Both laughed and she begged him not to tell her daughter or anyone yet.

Kebba dare not spill the beans for aside being a very respectable elder in his sixties he has two other wives who would raise hell of a trouble for him not following tradition. Nonetheless the younger of the two wives suspected something brewing between Mary and Kebba by the smiles and the glances passing between him and Mrs. Marry Lovenut.

She alerted friends who discovered nothing to confirm her fears. Their snooping came to no avail before the young jealous wife rested her oars about her husband's clandestine relation with Mary. Mean while the secrete lovers opened up to each other with Kebba bringing forth his polygamous life and there was no way he would divorce the other ladies if Marry decided to be his third wife. This was all right with him and he assured her that the other ladies in his life concord with the tradition and would all in the power of tradition accept her and make her a comfortable sister in sharing him.

In all fairness Mary Lovenut was left bewildered. She grew in a place where monogamy was the dictum nothing more and nothing less than it. She needed to share feelings but it was too soon to share this bit with her newly married daughter. Her flight back to United Kingdom was in forty-eight hours time.

She asked to meet with Kebba again and indeed they had another go at sex only this time it lasted longer with her getting multiple orgasms as all were busy at the farms. This was some thing she missed since the passing of her late husband. She confessed Kebba to be better love match for her.

She savored every moment of him and would not want him to stop giving it to her. It was during this second encounter that she boldly asked if Kebba would mind marrying a white lady in her fifties who would certainly not reward him with a child. Kebba said, "In Africa we marry because we love not how one looks or what may come out of the marriage.

Children are a gift from the Almighty God and will come when He wills it. That was not a worrying thing to me but I am concern as to whether you can blend into such a different culture at this day of your life. I do understand you have come to love me. I strongly advice you reflect upon my proposal to marry you when in England. Where possible discuss it with your daughter before replying.

I will always love you despite answer you may arrive at." They hugged and kissed and went back to the villa where Kunsa and Jane had been wondering what held the two from joining them at dinner. Jane dished out Foofu and palm oil and cassava leaf source with lots of meat in it which they gorged themselves to the throat.

However their feet kept rubbing on each other under the dining table to a point Jane noticed and smiled knowing that something heartwarming had happened for mother on her Gambian trip.

Soon Kebba left for home to be with his wives and the moment Jane and Kunsa moved upstairs to their bedroom they laughed and each tried to reveal what he or she noticed going on between Mary and uncle Kebba. Kunsa begged Jane not to let his uncle know that they knew what transpired until he brings it up.

It will keep his pride intact. Jane promised not to discuss it with her mum but was certain that if there was any momentum in it her mum would call to share her feelings as well ask for advice on how to go about it. She added, "I knew about it two days ago but did not want to embarrass you about your uncle's escapes with her beyond middle age mother.

We must wait for them to open the Pandora's box at a time suitable to them. Agreed?" Very soon Marry's mobile phone rang and at the other end was Kebba. He said, "Hello darling. I am already missing while you are in Gambia. How will I cope when you leave tomorrow morning?

Love is at times not fair as it hurts at the wrong time. I have told my wives about you because I want all of you to be able to trust my word and not see me as a double standard fellow who talks from one side of his mouth while not meaning a word uttered by him. I love you and would marry you if you do accept to be my third wife. I will be at the airport to see you off hoping that you will keep your promise of calling as soon as you arrive. Darling, I will miss you dearly, Sweet dreams."

They kissed the longest kiss on the phone and Mary went to bed straight not knowing that Jane and Kunsa were listening to the entire conversation on their intercom speaker. They were happy about the unfolding elderly love and candor of uncle Kebba.

Jane summed the experience telling Kunsa, "I wish our European men were this forth right with their feelings and plans for executing them in appropriate manner while considering all those in involved in the jigsaw." It was a bright Saturday with sparkling blue skies. There were no clouds to be seen as far as Senegal and cool Westerly winds kept the temperature down.

Uncle Kebba and Mary Lovenut rode at the back of the limo. They could not avoid holding hands leading the young driver to ask, "When did you too meet?" They laughed and released their grips, which alerted the nosey driver. The glances and occasional kisses in the air pervaded and continued through the 16 miles trip to Yundum International Airport.

This was the most difficult time for the lovebirds as all eyes were fixated on every move they did. But alas! Kebba risked and hugged Mary while wishing her bon voyage. He told her to write, of course meaning to call as soon as she landed at Heathrow. Mother like daughter had a dream experience she was not about to relinquish to any one no matter who may be objecting her intended move and plans to marry Kebba while accepting polygamy as **status co in Africa. Mary boarded the BA Flight heading for the UK with misty eyes and already planning her return trip to the Gambia the moment she set foot in the plane. She had spent most of her early vacations in either Tenerife or the West Indies but never in Africa.**

This trip was an eye opener that helped her throw all diatribe huller-hoes about Africa and the natives. She was going to cling hard onto opportunity about to knock at her door. As agreed between her and uncle Kebba she called the moment she cleared her luggage at Heathrow International before taking the National Express to Manchester.

Kunsa had bought a new I pod for his uncle Kebba and when it went burr, burr, burr, he was unable to answer as he placed all his fingers on surface of the screen. It was Kadija who came to his rescue by dialing the number that was calling.

Mary answered, "Hello, darling, I am home but missing you and feeling lonely without you. Please hang up and I will ring back immediately to safe you from a very expensive call." Kebba did as commanded and soon the call followed. This time he did the correct thing and heard Mary's voice loud and clear as if she were a few feet away. He marveled at the white man's

technology and asked, "When will Africa be as efficient as this toy in my hand?" He told her, "I too missed you very much but I remain hopeful that the solitude would be of a short lived type. I am looking forward to seeing you on your return trip in two months time."

Mary confirmed her aspiration of making the relationship work for both of them and that she would arrange to have her home rented out and the money will help in her resettlement in the Gambia. It can help in the refurbishing existing building at home of Kebba and also build one or two additional villas to current blockhouses he and her mates lived in.

This said. Uncle Kebba kissed over the phone and promised never to let her go away from his sight. He was so happy that he begged her to return sooner. Mary said, "Darling, haste makes waste. We must take things with reasonable speed and not rush through our plans, as that will land us in an abyss.

I will need to discuss the house with my solicitors, talk to my daughter and her uncle about us and buy us material we would need at the home in the Gambia. I will get a standby generator to make certain we have electricity all day or when needed."

She paused to allow Kebba absorb the details and put forth any suggestions he might have. Kebba could only just say, "Thank you for being so generous and utterly lovely. You will not regret your investment in our lives. Part of me is already in England and please come soon for me to be the whole unit that I was for all of you."

Mary in much lighter mood asked, "How on earth do you manage to satisfy all of us without crumbling for good?" Kebba laughed and said, "That is the African male's time honored secrete.

All you need is a very good sex any time it comes to your turn in revolving wheel of polygamy." His voice alone was enough to set Mary into orgasm. Luckily she was alone at the rare of the bus and no one heard her groans as this male's voice set her pouting. Kebba had to go for some visitor wanted to talk to him about problem he was having at his house. The lovebirds kissed and said their goodbyes before hanging off.

Mary ruminated and reflected over the good times she had with her sixty-year-old African male in the Gambia of all places. The National Express bus arrived in Manchester after five hours and her brother who was eager to visit the Gambia when he takes his leaf in three months time picked Mary from the station.

On the way to Parkland Road he asked several questions about the people, their friendliness, and interesting things to see and buy and about ladies. Mary painted an even rosier picture than he already had from his nice Jane."Sis, he said, rest assured I am in a hurry to set foot in the Gambia.

I hope you got a good bloke to keep you company?" Mary was tempted to open up then and there and tell him about all the good experience her new found love in Kebba. Instead she only smiled and asked, "Rob, will you be able to drop by for a cup of coffee and family chit-chat 6.30 pm on Saturday?"

Of course Robert was eager to hear more about the Gambia and what his sister observed and brought back. He said in true Brit way, "Mary, see you 6.30 pm Saturday." He helped Mary lift heavy pieces she brought and then left horridly to join his friends at the pub a mile away.

Mary unpacked her things and took a quick shower before fixing a cup of hot tea and milk, with bread and marmalade spread on it. Her mind ran into the last moments she had with Kebba and even the thought of it was delicious and percolates her heart with love. She felt like a sixteen year old girls just returning from her first date with one she was dying to be with. She held the hatful cup high in the air sang and danced round and round the table only to be disturbed ringing of her mobile. It was Jane calling to find out if she finally settled and rested in cold Manchester.

Mary replied, "I am fine but just want to come back right away. I am missing you a lot being in diary Manchester. There is no fund for people of my age in this god foreshaken cold weather and youth oriented country of ours. No wonder we indulge in lot of alcohol consumption and mischievous ventures to keep us realized.

It is an unnecessary attention calling and looseness coming to see it from the point of outsiders. We play too much into merciless hands of the cosmetic industry, which dictates the look rather than the heart and communal life. How are you and the baby faring?

You must be happy having Kunsa a husband. There is something I want to discuss with you tomorrow evening. Would that be all right? I am still unpacking. Thank you love and speak to you tomorrow. Good night."

Jane told Kunsa of her mother's possible readiness to open the Pandora's box about her love relation with uncle Kebba. Kebba had recently frequented their home and enquiring about Mary.

Kunsa said, "What God brought together cannot be defrayed. Perhaps the two families were meant to be one and I will do all I can for Mary and Kebba to arrive at their wish to be a couple. However as a mark of respect traditional norms require us keep it to ourselves until invited by them."

Jane promised not to let the cat out until when appropriate for society. Had it been in England she would be on the bullhorn (mobile) blabbing her mother's secrete to all her friends just to draw attention to herself.

Not so in Africa, there are many other important things to occupy oneself with during the day than endless empty chit-charts. There is work, children husband and mates to deal with in a fluctuant communal environment short of many basic necessities taken for granted in Europe and America.

The next and almost went before the phone rang. It was Mary. Kunsa picked it and said, "Hello mum! How are you and the weather in Manchester?" She said, "Fine and you?" Kunsa told they were all right and eager to hear from her as they are missing her already. And then handed the phone over to Jane, who asked him to put on the speaker for Kunsa to hear what Mary had in mind.

She then said, "Hi mum. I hear you loving wintry Manchester. How is Uncle Rob?" "We are fine and happy for you and Kunsa. My call is in regards to uncle Kebba, about whom I am sleepless and restless for want of being in his arms again.

I love him and asked if you being his nephew's wife and my daughter would condone such relationship and would it offend Kunsa?" Jane said, "Mum, this is the greatest news I ever had in my life. It is like Santo Claus bringing the most coveted gift for me. I am so happy to know your relation and attraction to uncle Kebba.

I am delighted and have no objection what so ever as long as it's not one of those menopausal instincts to feel being woman again. Marriage here involves family and community.

Would you be able to share your husband with other wives senior to you?" Mary reassured her daughter by revealing that aspect has been thoroughly dealt by her and Kebba, who even told his other two, wives his intention to marry her as his third wife.

They welcomed the move and promised to treat her as a sister taking care of Kebba and family. It was at this point that Jane asked if her mum would like to speak to Kunsa about her joy. She was happy to do. Kunsa took the set and pretended not having heard a word of what transpired between mother and daughter. "Hello mum.

Jane just told me part of the good news but I want to hear from the horse's mouth to be certain and push for things move faster than normal." Mary summarized things thus, "I met Kebba and instantly fell in love with him and he with me.

We have discussed our feelings for each other and arrived at the decision to marry and my daughter has assured me of her support and I have no doubt of your helping Kebba and I wed. Is there any reason for objection from his family or community that he was embarrassed revealing because of his love for me?

I love him dear and would be willing and happy to adapt to marital norms of your culture. Kebba went in great length in clarifying things for me. Do not hesitate or think that you will hurt my feeling by telling the natty-gritty of life under or in the Mandinka tradition."

She paused to hear Kunsa's response. He reinforced his commitment saying, "Uncle Kebba is a respected person and hence would not do anything that would tarnish his reputation. This is reason why he brought the other wives into the picture from the onset of your relations.

He revealed all that transpire to them to gain their respect and true participation in his intention to marry you. We are hundred percent in support of the move. Once you commit yourself to do it purely from love's point of view then only joy awaits you.

Come we will be your pillars With Jane back on the phone Mary said, "I cannot wait to come and hug my in-law for being so truthful and direct about things. I now have confidence to discuss my intentions with Rob on Saturday. I also plan to take him to the Mahal Mos Doli restaurant you took me the last time.

I am certain it will be an eye opener for him because he believes food and vegetables from Africa are not worth for pig's consumption more over civilized being like the Brits. I am very relieved that you agree with me and be reassured that it is not postmenopausal infatuation or wanting to be lady again. I am fifty-four years old but I am fully cognizant of my acts and decisions I make.

My card is almost gone. Good by and good night. I will speak to on Saturday after discussions with Robert. Bye for now." Jane was delighted but wondered whether her uncle Bob would encourage her because of opinions he expressed openly on several times whenever the topic was about Africa and African.

He sees the African as lazy bunch of illiterates dressed in leaves and enjoy life in shanty homes or mud house instead of house made breaks and mutter. They still have ancient modes of transport i.e. the mule, dugout canoes and use bows and arrows to hunt. Jane could not see how Uncle Rob could make a u-turn from such ingrain fallacies he has about Africa but it was worth for her mother to try sound him out.

Knsa consoled by telling her that not long ago she encountered similar resistance from uncle Kebba who is today a convert. The same bug could just sting her uncle Rob to see things differently. "You never know how far your uncle would opt for reconciliation to bring happiness to your mum who has been single for ten years after the death of your father.

He has already told you about his interest to visit the Gambia shortly. That alone is a change in the right direction. Be happy Kebba will soon be our uncle and father in law." The two laughed at that hugged and went to as it was getting late. Jane had a busy day waiting at the MRC laboratory.

Mean while Robert was at Mary's doorstep at 6.30 pm prompt. Mary was taken by surprise because Rob had no previous no respect for time or appointment which he seem to make it his just flaunt. "Come in, Mary said. "Take a seat at the table or settee while I prepare us some coffee." She joined with two cups of tea, bread and marmalade.

They took few sips before she broke the looming silence. "Rob I call to talk to you about me. You know women at my age in England seen as nothing old bags for glut of young ladies in the street. I have been widowed for almost ten years and life has become intolerably lonely for me.

However, I found my knight in Gambia and want your advice before I move too far and fast into relationship or marriage." Mary was embarrassed to amid that things have indeed gone beyond level she was willing to reveal to her younger brother now a full grown man. Robert said, "Sis, tell me real details about this man and how you met ant what you know about him and his tribe.

You know how I feel about those natives in the jungles of Africa." This sent a shivers in Mary's spine for she wants no fight about her love to Kebba with his only living relative. She calmly said, "Well, I met Kebba, who is uncle to Kunsa, and we instantly fell for each other.

He was very forthright about his feelings for me but gave me the option to opt out in the event that I do not nurture same love for him. He said he would be hurt but will never stop loving me in his heart. It was he who told me to return o the UK and reflect on it before giving my final commitment to marriage."

Now you being the only male relative I have left what is your take on this door that opened for me in the Gambia?" Robert held his head between his hands for a while then said, "Sis, you and have been frank to each other since childhood and I sincerely thank you for opening up and my answer is simple.

If you do love this fellow as much as seem to show in your purports then I only wish the best for the two you. You have my full support to go ahead on whatever level you want your relationship reach.

It was not until when Jane made that move that made me like and respect blacks than I ever did in my life. Report coming from those who visited and interact with the indigenous of Africa, especially the Gambia, spoke well of them and their readiness to share the little they have to make people like you and I have good time in their homes is a cheerful.

You have to make arrangements to care for the house if the two of you marry. You would need to let an agency take over and rent the house for you. This will be another source of a guaranteed income to fall back onto on a rainy day. Again, congratulations and I am with you all the way to the bridal lane in the Gambia." Both sister and brother laughed and hugged amid tears in their eyes. Yes, it has been ten lonely and difficult years of waiting for Mr. Right to show for Mary.

The two let to have dinner at the Gambian restaurant on Winslow Rod, Manchester. On taking their table she ordered Benechin, Yassa, Chakrri and lots local soft drinks made in Gambia. At first Rob was squeamish but seeing her sister delves into her bowl of benechin he too gave it a try and like it so much.

He finished his in no time and asked a bigger portion to in replenishing his bowl. He tried the Chakkrri and spooned all of it in few moves. Rob turned to Mary and said, "Sis, why do people over here tell us rubbish about food and vegetables coming from Africa?

This so far is one of the most delicious meals I ever had in my entire life. I am heading for the Gambia in two moths time and I will be me a beautiful dame if cook as good as dished in this restaurant. Everyone laughed and raised their glasses full of Mango juice tossed to him and his forthcoming trip.

"Sis, Rob, continued we in the so-call developed world drink excessively and fight at pubs while the people over there in Gambia and developing countries that we thumb ours noses upon enjoy life and nature better than us. Jane and the Gambians have no doubts opened another window of positivism my life had lack until today."

Rob continue talking to the next table close to him and was Eve in more delighted by the number that had been to the smiling coast of Africa and how they fell in love with the people, especially villagers.

After trying two cups of Ataya, a highly caffeine charged brewed leafs with lot of sugar and milk added, Rob and Mary drove home. At Mary's house he said, "Sis, thanks for a love night. I am heading home as it is getting late. Again, I am hundred percent behind your desire to wed uncle Kebba.

Rest assured of that sis." Mary, a robust, fit and witty, stunning fifty-year-old lady with deceptive looks of a thirty-eight lady meditated on her coming new life and changes it required. Anxiety prompted her to call Jane first thing in morning and asked how she was coping and if she still believed her marrying uncle Kebba was right for her.

Jane assured her mum saying, "Mum, I am fully in support of you but the paramount thing is love and sincerity to one's commitment. One man's meat could be another's poison. Hence, do not base your move predicated to mine. That would be a fatal mistake on your part.

 I happen to accidentally meet a man I loved and love me dearly if not more than I expected. I have him and found actions of him, his family, relatives and friends in making life jolly for us exceptional. The decision is yours alone and we will support you whichever way you choose to go about it. Have you spoken to Uncle Rob about your crush for uncle Kebba?

What was his opinion about it?" Mary was quick to point out that she was not about to back out from her feeling for Kebba but to make certain that she still had all onboard after letting the cat loose and allowing time for them to think over the ramifications that may surface. Mary told her daughter to brace up for a new fantastic step dad, making Jane laugh. Mary said, "Please extend my greetin Kunsa and uncle Kebba." That week Mary went into a mega-shopping spree of buying dining tables, chairs, computers, sofas, plasma TV and lot of presents for Kebba's two other wives. At the end she had a full twenty-foot container to ship to the Gambia before her final journey there.

Gambia became Mary's home away from her birth land home. On landing at Yundum International Airport, she was met by jubilant elderly ladies in colorful traditional dress send to start her bridal trail. She was whisked into a convoy of limo as soon as arrival formalities were completed.

She was allowed to talk to Jane who further assured her that the saga she was going through was enactment of millions of years of tradition of the Mandinka tribe in Gambia, Guinea, Mali and Senegal. Mary's connubial link to Kebba would take a quitter nature compared to that of Jane.

The reason for this low profile being that Kebba and Mary had previous marriages before tying today's knot between them. Hence at sunset, four elderly ladies cheerfully walked Mary to cross the bridal thresh whole. She met uncle Kebba in his best traditional dress seating on the bed waiting for her first steps in being his legal wife. The elderly escort shut the door behind them and headed home.

The bride and bridegroom continue where they had long before tying the knot. In the morning told of a very happy honeymoon and that Kebba said to her "Never let me go." Kebba's other wives accepted Mary as their sister. Her big day bloomed to many happy years thereafter and she never regretted having married Kebba. All is well that ends well. Mary's dream holiday turned a bonanza she never ever expected in her fifty years of life. Gambia is a tiny country with physical beauty and historic links with Brits. Almost by miracle Gambia's exposure as a holiday destination brought it into high rank of International Mecca of tourism.

Jane and Mary wrapped with love the force of nature, were pleased with their Gambian encounter proving worthiness in people visiting their global neighbors. You are always welcomed to the Gambia, the smiling coast of Africa.

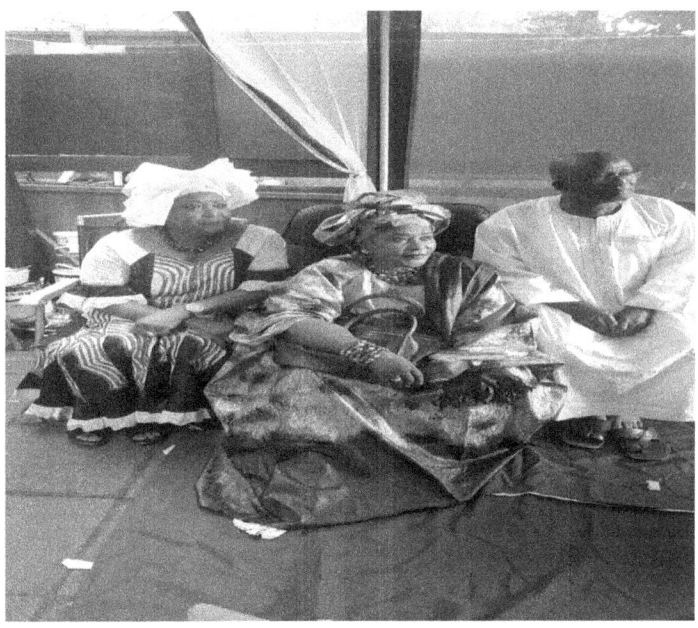

L-R: Sukai Bouvier Sali Darbo Kebba Dampha 2017

The Sunshine of My Life

Love like light brightens life. The romantic flood we are about to witness by the presence of stunning Musu Koyo Fati and tall, broad-shouldered man with a pleasant face, Sambu Kinte tells endless wonders of love. It was back in the 1950s at Kinte Kunda village that our saga commences.

Musu was born on the 14th of February while Sambu landed on the Garden of Eden on the first of January 1950. One was a valentine dream goddess and the other a most welcomed blessing of the year and good omen for his childless parents.

Much more relates to these fledgling villagers, as their parents have been historically long time friends, their fate would be wound and intertwine in the most cherished and envied way to their compatriots. Legend had it that the two children did start primary school seating side by side at Kinte Kunda Primary School.

They in fact competed very fiercely for grades and for having answered most questions asked by the teacher in any subject at the time. Musu's attending school in the fifties was an unheard of role or phenomenon. Most parents rather have their daughters groomed in the ancient traditions than dabbling with strange Western cultures and schooling, which they considered as grievous waste of the girls' time and future.

Sambu and Musu tethered on without any inclination of romance between them up to the forth year when they separated as Sambu Kinte continued his schooling at St. Augustine Secondary while Musu Koyo's parent were contended in her attending Armitage Secondary School at George Town, some 175 miles away from Kinte Kunda.

What magical warn was there that would united these ambitious student? First Sambu turned to be a brilliant student that got A grade in most the subject he took at the Advance GCE level and was later offered scholarship to read for a degree in economics.

Miss Musu Koyo Fati too never looked back. She got her A levels in the Sciences and was sent to UK to read for a medical degree. Sambu returned a well-grounded economist and was appointed Permanent Secretary Ministry of Finance; Dr. Musu Koyo Fati was eventually appointed head of the Pediatrics Units and CEO of the Royal Victoria Hospital in Banjul, Gambia's capital.

The duo never ceased corresponding and becoming civil servants in the same city further encouraged linkage as they frequently met at government seminars on administration and women empowerment.

No, this would not be the venue were the ice would be broken for these fiercely ever competing civil servants. Three months lat both were invited to attend a banquet in behalf a visiting dignitary to the Gambia. The president of Sierra Leone,

Mr. Good Fortune was on a three days working visit at the end of which Gambia's president offered to entertain his friend and brother from Free Town, the Diamonds and Palm whines state of West Africa. The quick sands of romance reared it tantalizing head when Sambu, to Musu's surprise, walked straight to her and ask her to dance with him.

She obligingly accepted and indeed they danced perfectly with nimbleness of nymphs and darling angels. It was during that close encounter that the two felt something very strong and enamor about each other. Sambu Kinte could not stop looking into her big lovely eyes and wishing that he never let her out of his sight. She in return just smiled and asked what took him so long to take heart to be kind to her.

She said, "I have dreamt of this dance over and over and even refused to be engaged to a fellow Gambian doctor over in the United Kingdom. The thought of you dominated my dreams and wish. Having said this I hope you will not be infatuated by this frank declaration.

I am not good at going round about my feelings and it has been about love for you since our primary school days." Dr. Musu Koyo paused to let things sink and have its effect. Sambu Kinte being beaten to the post and seriously overwhelmed could only thank his stars.

He said, "My dearest Musu, I must confess that I have never had any girl in my heart and daily thought than you. I have written poems and songs about you but your brave step has made me look peevish for not taking the bull by the horn earlier than today."

The music stopped to allow the host to give a brief speech and a reply by his visiting brother politician. Musu and Sambu walked hand in hand and at peace for the first time since primary school to their seats a few rows apart. Nonetheless they kept throwing romantic glances and smiles conjunct with air kisses.

Soon the MC of the night jokingly announced, "Would the gentlemen engage their ladies for this is a special tune for lovers." Undoubtedly many men rushed to engage pretty

Dr.Musu Koyo Fati, which she rebuffed unabashed until her knight, Permanent Secretary for Finance Mr. Sambu Kinte elbowed his way among the throng vying for her.He said, "Darling, can we continue were we stopped the last time? The dance floor waits."

Dr. Musu smiled. Said why not?" Followed him to the center and during a slow dance they charted and talked about the future and how it could be a bright illuminating one for them and their children. It was then that Sambu Kinte told her of his impending mission to England for two weeks but would miss her dearly.

She assured him by saying, "Have no worries for I have waited as long as has been the case. Your being away for two weeks would not kill either one of us. You must be very careful not to be hooked by those fast white girls in England."

Sambu Kinte laughed but took the last bit very seriously knowing that she dose harbor jealous feelings and that he has to make sure he gave her something that allays her fears. The night went well. Placed the ring on her finger and hugged him.

After series of long kisses, she declared, "I took The two decided to have some soft drinks at the Boka hol restaurant, meaning heart unites; were they ironed out their plans and arranged to meet after 7.30 pm the next day at the supper benechin take away not far where Musu lives.

Sambu Kinte went to the jewelries and bought the highest-grade diamond engagement ring and also a fresh bouquet of red rose placed them in brown bag to meet Dr. Musu Fati at the above venue. On taking their seat at a quiet corner Sambu Kinte pulled the ring and roses from the bag. He knelt and in a simple moving way, and said, "Darling, I too have dreamt of today and I am with all there is in me asking you to be my wife if you equally have the same feeling for me. I assured you of my love and would provide and as well protect you, our children and all that belongs to our extended family and us.

I would be the luckiest of man for wining your heart and for being father of our children. Again, please accept this ring which is far below your worth in my heart." Dr. Musu, with misty eyes got up as he love you and would be proud of being your wife and mother of your children.

I will be by your side in thick and thin throughout my life. My love for you is infinite and I would like you know that you are the sunshine of my life and anything I live for. I am happier than happiness by your finally braving the romantic waters that had been bobbling between us since our primary days at Kinte Kunda."

Again they kissed raising the attention of onlookers and the staff who applauded them amid songs and cheering. After another half an hour Dr. Musu's blip went on indicating that she had to break the meeting for the Pediatric Registrar on night call needed her. She gave a quick kiss and Sambu saw her off to her car.

He returned to pay the bills and went home very happy that his dream lady was from henceforth finally found. While ruminated on a line from Shakespeare' work came to mind. It ran, "Cowards die twice before their death." Yes, Sambu felt ashamed that he kept his feelings for Dr. Musu Koyo Fati as long as it did.

He too wanted to read for a medical degree but was nudged to economics because no scholarship was available for him and the Colonial Secretary recommended him reading for an economic degree. Dr. Musu attended to her duties and then called Sambu. "Hello honey, what has just happen is life you have to adapt to. A doctor's life is literally chained to his or her patients which ties confuse most husbands.

Are you certain my work will not come between the good doors we have just opened for each other?" Sambu reply saying, "Thank God we have similar engagements. I am certain and be rest assured that it will never be a hindrance for I know the duties and life of professionals like us. Who would like to lose such delicious love for frivolous but real office hours?

You must accept and know that life must be ruled by the dictum God before duty and duty before pleasure for one to reward oneself and society. Is it not fact that I will be away for two weeks from Monday? Thank you for claming and calming my fears," replied Dr. Musu. They charted like teenagers into the wee hours of the night with either one not wanting to end it despite workload waiting at the office the next day.

They were so hungry to spill their guts out to each other in hallow of romance. They have never had such cheerful life and wished that every second found them glued to each other. Their love grew exponentially. Dr. Musu took three hours off to see Permanent Sectary Sambu Kinte accompanied by his boss to fly to London on a mission. She watched the metal take off toward temperate cloud veiled London.

She went to her office laden heart already longing for Sambu Kinte. Alas, she braced up and worked hard and longer than ever to mask solitude his travels and physical absence brought to her life. She never felt like that before their opening up to each other but she now almost think of Samba daily with hope that each telephone call would be his. She wrote on her notebook, "NO one had ever been left on their feet on coming across Mr. Right or their knight on a white horse ready to gallop with them to coveted bridal lanes.

Oh, dearest Sambu I am all yours like a plumb waiting to be eaten. I will hang on for thee for no one will sway my heart away from you." Three days later Sambu called from his hotel in London. "Honey, I miss you dearly. How are you? We had series of marathon meeting keeping me on my toes nearly all day through half the night.

We are progressing in getting some help from here. What would you like me bring for you when coming?" Dr. Musu delighted to hear his voice said, "Nothing other than you. I am dying to be with you. I hope you are wrapping up well to ward off the Manchester cold weather.

Again do not look at the girls over there. Remember I studied in Manchester and I am very familiar with cheap life some Africans lead in that city. I have to go. My blip is on again. I will call you later to night. Love you, bye for now." Sambu would have preferred they had a longer chart but duty would not let her.

He looked forward to her call latter at night. This was the first Sambu ever had to Britain or the European Union and so far he was very impressed with what he saw and how the machinery of government operates in the United Kingdom. They have two free days by the end of the visit, which he planned to tour London tourist sites including London Bridge, Westminster Cathedral and Buckingham Palace to watch changing of the guard, which had impressed him on seeing it since his high school days. Seeing it live would leave an indelible image in his memory of the trip to UK. Dr. Musu called as promised eager to hear how Sambu's day went. She said, "Darling, another week away will farce me to take a sick leave and join you in England."

Both laughed and she told him how she misses him and work load she took just to let time fly away. She said, "Without your presence life has become an empty void. Please come back as soon as possible." Sambu promised to do just that because he too was equally missing her.

Time flew fast and Sambu Kinte toured interesting places and bought a brand new two door Mercedes Benzes and choked it presents for Dr. Musu Koyo Fati. He had it shipped right away. The permanent Secretary and entourage flew back to the Gambia at the end of two weeks hard work.

He was very happy heading towards the goddess of his heart. Sure enough five and half hours after leaving Manchester Airport Sambu Kinte landed safely at Yundum International Airport in the Gambia. He found Dr. Musu Koyo waiting for him at the VIP lounge. They kissed, and kissed, and kissed like teenagers given ice cream after a desert field trip.

After the formalities to two rode in Sambu Kinte's black limo and headed straight to his home where they up dated and caught up with developments in their lives. It was during this private tête-à-tête that they finalized when to tie the nut and where it should take place. Kinte Kunda Janeya was the venue and the wedding would be two months from that day.

All formalities and dowry was taken care of in no time and dignitaries, relatives, friends and well-wishers joined Sambu and Musu at their wedding in Kinte Kunda, Lower District. It was memorable and typical Mandinka wedding ceremony. Believe it or not the day of the honeymoon was the first time these lovebirds had sex. It enhanced trust in them for being virgins.

The two were given three weeks leave notice in which they spent part in Paris and the USA, a country they have always wanted to visit. Dr Musu returned carrying her first baby and Sambu became an expectant father. He was surprise at strength women had in them.

Dr. Musu kinte continued her normal duties even when she was eight months pregnant. Unlike habit of most gestating female senior civil servants, Dr. Musu Kinte selected delivering her baby at the Royal Victoria Hospital where other Gambian ladies had their babies.

Her reason being that if indigenous wealthy Gambians and senior civil servant shone the service available to ordinary people then that service was not worth name it carries and as far as she was concerned officials are duty or patriotically bound to develop the country's health services. The baby was named after the first president of the Gambia, Kairaba Kinte. Yes, the old statesman was delighted and gave a lot to the ceremony.

He further offered to sponsor the boy's university education even if he were not around. He would draw legal papers to that effect. The doctor and her husband lived very long happy years of marriage lasting fifty years before Musu passed away leaving old man Sambu Kinte in solitude and missing her dearly. He promised to never let her out of his heart.

Why Was Man Late Swallowing the Forbiden Apple?

It is alleged that Adam had to eat the forbidden apple to drag us into endless need for relationship. In the green days of love only angels sang to sooth the heart. Not now! Eve needing to procreate cajoled poor Adam into swallowing the forbidden fruit, believed to be an apple to cause him to be attracted to her.

In saga we are about to sail through we are lead to the impatient romance of a certain Miss Hadi Faye as her hormones would not let her rest in peace since sighting handsome Cherno Jobe, a teacher at Malfa Primary school in Banjul, the Gambia, West Africa.

Hadi Faye taught English and arithmetic at the Mohammedan School in Banjul and only came across Mr. Cherno Jobe at a teachers' annual symposium at the great hall of the people in Sere Jobe Kunda. They initially had heated argument about certain books to be introduced in the curriculum of schools of which Cherno Jobe thought to be degrading and would lower the standard of education.

Hence it must not be adopted but need to be thrown away. Hadi Faye on the other hand reminded the group that the Mr. Jobe was rejecting a good and simple book only because the author was his former schoolmate and later ex-girl friend. She warned him not to drag his personal feeling for the author to deprive the good it would have or bring to beginners.

At the end of the day Hadi carried the motion by an overwhelming majority present at the meeting. Mr. Jobe, a male chauvinist by nature bowed away with some trepidation but was not unnerved by the outcome.

He instead planned to swing Hadi Faye's heart to his favor by testing the will of this lady orator/talker that derailed him so smoothly. Hadi was an articulate, beautiful and intelligent lady. There were no doubts that had her parents been reached she would have been one bright PhD star among the Gambian academics.

Cherno Jobe was also a handsome science teacher of many years experience. Both never married and this firing line they shared at the meeting seems to draw them closer than was expected. Cherno dared the storm by calling Hadi and asking her out for a dinner, literally creating a chance for the two to have a proper private tête-à-tête away from gossipers.

Hadi obliged stating the rule thus; "I will come hoping that you have a mature proposition to offer instead of arguing childishly out of selfishness because your former ex had notoriety and is contributing in educating our children." Cherno Jobe who was expecting an outright denial was quick to say, "Darling, your wish is my command.

I just had this burning desire to share my heart with you. That said we meet at the Boka Holl Restaurant by 7:00 pm tonight. Would that be ok with you?" Hadi Faye replied, "It is perfect with me. I look forward to sharing the evening with you hopping that you have not swallowed the forbidden apple."

This made Cherno Jobe to laugh and say, "Well, dear, it was Eve who coaxed Adam to partake the apple at the Garden of Eden. I am eager to share delicious meal with you. See you at the Boka Holl shortly." Hadi being a very independent lady turned down Cherno's offer to take her to the restaurant in his Fiat car.

She hailed a taxi and made it to the venue the same time Cherno was parking his car. She walked to reception, selected a table at one of the quite corners of the restaurant and left a note for Cherno Jobe to join her when he makes it in.

Cherno's entrance was greeted with chorus of jokes from quite a few in the restaurant denoting his familiarity with place. Hadi's note was handed to him and he headed directly to her brimming smiles. On taking his seat directly facing her he asked, "What would madam like to eat or drink?

Have no worries I will take care of the bill." Hadi said, "Over my dead body. We will split it fifty-fifty between us or I move to my own table." She was still reeling at his chauvinistic attitude and she was not going to take that from him. Cherno calmed and said, "Okay, fifty-fifty." He called, "Waiter!"

A beautiful smartly dressed waitress with a broad smile came and said, "Good evening. What would Mr. and Mrs. Jobe like to eat or drink? Have you looked at our menu yet?" Hadi paying no attention to assumption made by the waitress said, "I will have Basi Nyebe, Chakirr and Mango juice please."

Cherno ordered a bowl of benechin; some foofu and Ataya drink to go with. Thanking the waitress as she left to prepare the dishes for them. In the interim the duo sipped guava juice while at the same time examining the other without seeming to have done so.

Cherno deliberately let his feet rub against those of Hadi and she responded by placing hers' closer and tighter to his. They rubbed feet passionately several times. This testing of wills continues for five minutes before Hadi broke the silence and asked, "Have you had another girl friend since Kumba dumped you? Was it because of your being impotent or just a childish play boy?" Hadi, unlike being shy is one who does not mince her words and says exactly what she meant.

Cherno came clean and told her their separation was for neither reasons but sheer incompatibility amid minimal love. He took the opportunity to correct her on the point that he was objecting for her ex-lover's book being accepted.

He said, "Believe it or not after reading it several times I came to conclude that our children need better books than that which laid too much emphases or carbon copy of other cultures instead of writing about our own. I have since then started one where the characters are all Gambians and the stories based on real happenings in the Gambia.

Perhaps I was taken by my nationalistic instinct and hence did not put my point clear enough to get understanding of where I was coming from regarding her work. It will be perfect for Europe but not for any African country." This statement of clarification impressed Hadi Faye and made her want to know why people think him chauvinist. He was as sweet and simple like anyone.

He just sticks his neck out for what he believes in and not a double standard in nature. Soon the conversation turned to the business of the day. Hadi said, "I have no male lover because I spent most of my time trying to perfect my lessons and in reality I have not met one until our argument at the meeting. I sensed something romantic in you but hated pushy males.

Now that you spill the beans, would you please accept my apology for challenging you in manner I did at the meeting. I find you very strong and attractive indeed. I hope you can say the same about me." Just when Cherno was about to say something the waitress interrupted him with a big tray containing their order for the evening. With all gingerly arranged and laid on the table she left the lovebirds to gorge themselves.

Cherno continued saying, "I too was drawn to you because of strange chemistry only akin with love. Yes, I love you and found you very beautiful, mature and attractive. I even told Samba Mbye, one of my best friends at the Treasury about you.

He was happy that I finally linked myself with one that was respectable and loved." They instinctively held hands amid gazing romantic eyes. Cherno wasted no time. He pulled from his pocket a diamond engagement ring and placed it on her finger, which caused tears of joys welling from Hadi's eyes.

He then added, "With this ring I want you to be my only wife for the rest of my life. I assure you my love, commitment to you and our children at all times. Hadi, dearest, please do say yes to me." All Hadi could say amid tears was, "Yes, yes! I am yours forever and I am more than happy to be your wife and mother of our children. Today, joy has reached my heart.

God guide our union." They kissed, had a few bites and left as night was creeping upon them with workload for the next day waiting to be cleared. This time they drove home with Hadi seated at the passenger side of Cherno's Fiat.On the way home Cherno said, "One of my dreams is about fulfilled for I did dream of our union many, many years ago when we first met at a debate in St. Augustine. I thank God for answering my prayers."Hadi girlishly looked at Cherno saying, "Darling, you have been a magnet to my soul since that great debate because of way you handled yourself and flawlessly presented your side of the topic. It was an impressive performance and a convincing quality of oratory gift.

In addition, I admit finding you very handsome, kind and strong man that attracted me to the core of my heart. I have loved you since but was not going to come forward to avoid looking like a bimbo to you. Hence, the reason why I never let your invitation to share meal with you at the Boka Holl go unheeded.

Now that the veil is off we must cement things and make up for lost time."It was at this junction that Cherno stopped slowly at Hadi's residence. She kissed him several times and alighted, walked to the door while taking last look and giving a flirting goodnight kiss towards him in the air.

Cherno sped away in delight he never felt since graduating from Yundum Teachers training College long time ago. It left him feeling like he was born again and much younger and energetic. It was not until after midnight did Hadi Faye called saying, "Dearest, I found it difficult to sleep without hearing your sweet voice.

I have finished preparing lessons for tomorrow's classes. I hope you had time to do yours. For the first time I felt like Eve did at the Garden of Eden because Adam was too slow in getting to eat the forbidden fruit. Please do not procrastinate about us. My feeling for you is too overwhelming darling. Rest assured your snakes are crawling all over me.

Again, Cherno told her that as of the following day he would send his relative to meet with her family in Banjul to set the ball rolling for the matrimonial union. They charted for an hour before accepting to hang up. The demeanor of both as noted by the pupils was very exhilarating.

They taught with unusual cheerfulness and excitement that made their pupils never wanted the lessons to end. The telephone rang right at break asking for Hadi Faye. She knew where the call was coming from and so she decided to take it from the next-door office away from listening ears. "Hi darling, how are you faring on with your students?

I just had to call for I could not stop thinking about you. My life is blessed with you in it." "Very well," replied Cherno, and the lessons went like breeze. I never felt so light and enjoying my work like it since we met. Thanks for bringing happiness into my life.

You are a unique rose of roses." Soon the school bell went off for the start of afternoon classes making the lovebirds scrambling for more time to talk more. On close of the day Cherno drove to Hadi Faye's school and took her home after a quick bite of delicious curry meal at the newly open All in one Take away franchised not far from Cherno's place.

Soon the cat came out of the bag and both schools were delighted of the forthcoming union of their best teachers. The students in her class along with staff at both schools were even more delighted for both of them than Hadi and Cherno ever expected for their pupils to show solidarity with a teacher. It was about end of term.

And guess what? The class decided to throw a party in her and Cherno's honour. On the day of the party, the school band provided music renditions ranging from Mbalah, Congolese songs, Motown, Diana Rose's "We will meet again" to Reggae, Wolof, Fulani and Manding music.

The staff brought gifts and flowers to serenade the soon would be couple. It was a touching affair and one of the most pleasant hours ever at the school. Everyone enjoyed him or herself and was eager to know the actual day of their tying the knot.

This they kept a guarded secret and each gave a heartfelt thanks to the staff and students for sharing the joy with them. Cherno promised to inform the school as soon as all formal decisions are ironed out traditionally. Many a heart have been brought together between staff but none matched the popularity and fanfare this one brought to the hearts of both teachers and pupils.

It was a one of rarity, which brought joyous welling tears from eyes of all attending it in the history of the two schools. Tingling pressures of love exhilarated the date of the wedding. Sure enough two weeks after the end of term Cherno and now Mrs.Hadi Jobe tied the knot at the grand mosque in Banjul.

The drumming and dancing went on for days while they flew to have their honeymoon to share the forbidden fruit at the Mayfair hotel in London. They toured London, visiting Westminster Abbey, Buckingham Palace, London Bridge and Tower along many interesting places of commerce. They return to Gambia with a twenty footer container full of all amenities they ever wished or lacked in the Gambia.

Soon Hadi broke the most welcomed news of being pregnant to her dearest man on earth. The baby boy came eight months later adding to the joy of life in Jobe kunda. The two continued their teaching professions and leaved happily for forty years before Cherno suffered a massive heart attack and returned peacefully to his maker. Man that ate the forbidden fruit was survived with three boys and two girls who all have grown up to be teachers and lawyers.

Alhagie Mama Ceesay Germany EU 2017

Love's Heydays

Back in 1978 young Fatou Kaloba would have led a normal girl's life at Manjie kunda had it not been her beauty and wildlife that sprouted petrifying attention. Fatou was a bewitching rose and glamorous figure whose luminous presence brought joy to her beholders. Some believed that her image and beauty turned her into the envy of angels.

Lang Marena was a humorous, generous and exciting and intelligent man whose heart sank for Fatou Kaloba. Fatou was nineteen years while Lang was in his early twenties. Both were in the green heydays of life and impelled into the most engaging romantic relationship. Their crossing path energized love.

They were vibrant, intelligent, happy, cheerful and very adventurous kids in love. They had no qualms with the way they felt for each other. They displayed raw love in spirit and in action. They were embodiment of the new romantic carefree generation.

Peers envy them while elders watched with admiration of their style of romance. Romance in the open was an unheard of expression in their days and to do so free to flaunt taboos was an admirable fit of bravery. At first Fatou's parents were blamed for her free lance attitude but folks soon came to respect Fatou kaloba because of dignity she carried her life with.

Even though nineteen years old she fed and provided money for the family by working at a nearby firm and was never seen to display or allow her turn to prostitution. She was just a vibrant human being doing her thing the way she saw fit without hurting others. Her forthrightness made her envied by her peers; most of who sort her advises when life seems to turn blue for them. Yes it was this magnet of an enigma that Lang Marena's heart went for at so early in their youthful life.

Lang taught at the Primary School a few kilometers away from Fatou's firm. The two only meet on weekends but more so during school holidays. There were no mobiles, Internet or telephones in their time and they had friends or younger kids to relay messages for them in the event they wish to rendezvous.

Despite their various professions they still help at the farm, which earned them much coveted respect from their community. It was amidst this admixture of life that the two set new romantic trend villagers only dreamt of but they dare not display. These lovebirds held hands and walked the streets together and kissed openly in broad daylight.

This was a social feat unseen or unheard of taking place with being lynched by so-called demigods of taboos. An elderly octogenarian met Lang and asked, "Son where did you harvest your guts? If I were to do what you did today during my youthful day my parents would have banished me from the village for it was despised to see man and woman being so free and expressive of love without fear of reprisal.

I admire you for belling the cat and being free to express your feelings openly. I am happy to see freedom creeping into our lives in my lifetime. God bless your eventual union with ravaging and stunning Fatou Kaloba." Fatuo and Lang met on several weekends and had bicycle rides to villages drawing more attention and admiration.

Owning a bicycle in those days in villages was like having a Mercedes Benzes. Kids want to touch it and wonder how the rider balances on two wheels. So Lang and Fatou were always center of attention and yearning for many of their peers.

Even though romantic they were not the freaky type that would do offensive things like premarital sex, to hurt village norms. Lang Marena decided that Fatou reaching twenty was right time to settle and after a heart to heart discussion the two agreed for him to send his relative to Fatou's parents asking for their permit to marry their daughter.

Hence Uncle Fafa Marena and friends took the task of bringing these youthful hearts in union by traditional route of meeting the parents of the future bride. At the home of Musa Kaloba and wife Majula the guests were welcomed with offers of goat milk and kola nuts.

The emissaries after a lengthy salutation with their host came directly with business of the day and reason for their visit. Uncle Fafa Marena started by reiterating long historic ties between the two families and how he and Musa Kaloba were and had been close friends ever since.

At the end he said, "The Marena dynasty is before them for endearing cause as they stand for their son and nephew Lang Marena in seeking permission of the Kaloba family to allow Lang Marena to marry their lovely daughter Fatou Kaloba after completion of traditional prerequisites. We wish to continue where feasible,

Barring the chance of your having earmarked her for a distant relative, long history of linkage between the two families." Other delegates and distant relatives echoed similar sentimentalities regarding relation of the Marenas and the Kaloba family. All negotiations transpired in the entirety of amicable atmosphere allowing easy ironing out of the cost of dowry and presents for the future bride. Despite being in the early part of the twentieth century what was required of Lang's family amounted to one three year old healthy bull and a heifer, half a kilo of gold or diamond, a Radio, yes, radios in those days were luxury of the rich and not many villagers had one; special embroiled fabrics from Mali and things the bride would herself request.Fatou Kaloba was not a greedy lady and her love Lang Marena

Mrs. Binta Ceesay, Sister

surpasses earthly things she might rub her future life partner. Hence when asked what she demanded to be wed by Lang she replied, "I thank all present especially my parents for love extended and for giving me choice about the ensuing marvelous future between Lang Marena and I.

All I want is his unconditional love, protection of our children and the catering for extended families which would become even closer at the end of the day and history our two families. Love is priceless hence am asking for no earthly goods or gilders from him. Again thank you for bringing me up with love and good guardian."

This stunned the audience who in unison sang praises to her and promised her support and the best wedding the region will ever witness. She overwhelmed them with candor for it echoed family upbringing her parents pride themselves for. She was one of their good daughters and her demeanor before the group spoke well for her and the family.

All having been settled the delegation promised to return with all the above prerequisites for the marriage to take place in two months time. During this period both friends and peers of Lang Marena and Fatou Kaloba chipped in and collected more than asked for.

They were able to purchase two kilos of gold, three bulls, fifteen rams, a hundred goats and tones of special designed and embroiled fabric for the wedding dress and others as Fatou may see it fit. In addition Lang bought her a100-karat gold cum diamond ring for the wedding day.

The regional farmers also donated hundreds of shacks of rice, millet and coos-coos for guests to consume during the wedding ceremony. Yes, in African villages no event is of a one man or home's event. All gladly chip in to make it a fund and memorable occasion for the couple, family and community.

What one has in the bank does not apply for unsolicited input from the heart is the best depository. Two months to the day Fafa Marena and company delivered the goods at the center of Musa Kaloba's home. Again, after the greeting formalities and well wishes for good health and prosperity; the containers were opened, gold weighed, fabric taken with admiration of the quality and lastly the bulls were stationed at the backyard.

Fatou Kaloba was summoned to say if she still plans to wed Lang Marena. This she affirmed and her parents and relatives blessed her and accepted the agreed dowry before them. The elders offered a short prayer and then the kaloba scribe was then authorized to announce the engagement and subsequent wedding to follow between Lang Marena and Fatou Kaloba.

The high priest will sanctify the marriage after the Friday prayers at the grand mosque. This done the wedding ceremony would take place three weeks after to allow further preparations. On the coming of the coveted day the whole region poured into Njawara by the thousands if not more to join in celebration of youngsters that set a social trend that would never be reversed for gone are the days of hidden romances.

Now kids will kiss openly and freely in the street with their intended. Hence more and more young men and women came to watch their idols hitched. On that Friday, drumming, dancing and plain fund rang through from hamlet to hamlet. People enjoyed themselves and partake of the abundant delicious food at their disposal. Poets and scribes scrambled to put the event and trend it set into prospectus for the anal of history to bear. As for the bride she appeared very spectacular in her traditional bridal dress with gold necklaces and bangles worth a fortune according to village standards. She was true and true princess incarnated before the admiring crowd. Her smiles with flashing ivory white teeth petrified some men.

Her beauty shone like a rod of lightening. She was immaculate and ravishing to behold. The villagers loved her and sang praises while heaping flowers on her bridal trail. The bridegroom in his well starched and ironed, embodied haft and dress was equally admirable. The couple was just unique to behold.

They smiled and waved at all present. People danced at their feet and promised to name their first born after them. This is a great honor in village concepts and traditions. The dancing and merriment went on through all of Friday night to the wee hours of early Monday before the celebrant called it quit and looked forward to another as good as this that everyone accepted to be the best the region ever had for a long, long time. The couple went to Banjul their honeymoon returning a month later more happy than ever. Hence all is well that ends well.

Craving For Your Love

At times one comes across a person who personifies all that we look for in a partner or love. This character becomes our dream and yearning above all things. We long to be with him or her and daily crave dearly for the person to recognize our itching for them.

This is the story of two that for many, many years longed to be together but unexpected whims of events kept postponing that to happen. We are about to find out how they overcame strong cravings and finally tied the knot twenty years later.

Kumba Jallow and Samba Sowe had since high school days been attracted to each other but tribal taboos and subsequent locations, in the days when telephones were unheard of in villages, made it impossible for the two to cement their lives together.

Kumba Jallow graduated from the Gambia Teacher's training College and took up post some three hundred miles away from a Health Centre where Samba works as a Dispenser. The two lost contact but remained deeply etched in their minds.

Samba Sowe attempted to locate her but was told she married and moved to another borough. It was not the Kumba Jallow he was looking for but it was her name shake that got married. This wrong information misled Samba Sowe who went into severe depression for several months having believed that he lost his heart's darling.

In the same vein Kumba Jallow wrote poems and sang songs about the man she would give heart. She constantly asks people from the North if they perchance know or met her Samba Sowe. The golf widens year in year out as time passes by. Hearts got fonder but not yielding an inch.

The search intensified from both camps to no avail. It reached a state where Kumba Jallow dwindled to a pencil size for not being married to Samba. She rejected all suitors arranged or otherwise. For her it was either Samba Sowe or no marriage.

Some thought her to be a hermaphrodite while others just sees her as stark mad for insisting on being married to her figments of a man. Samba too kept his loyalty to Kumba Jallow and refused a pretty dame his uncle selected for him to marry. So he was branded a fool and eunuch which stigma he paid little attention knowing that his day would come sooner than most expected.

The years went fast and it is now almost fifteen years since the two last saw each other at a naming ceremony. Kumba's parents summoned the services of an exorcist to retrieve her from the demonic grip Samba Sowe had on her. All attempts failed as it only reinforced her love for him. Those who the Gods unite cannot be separated even by time.

It will take another three years before Kumba ran into one of her students who handed a note from Samba Sowe to her. The fellow just said, "Mama, a Doctor at the Health Centre some three hundred miles from here who was treating my grandpa met me and after a lengthy questioning asked me to give you this envelope.

He would like to hear from you if you are person he believed we discussed at length." Kumba Jallow received the coveted envelope with trembling hands and an upsurge of relief she never experienced. Kumba opened the envelope and strait away recognized the writing and signature to be that of her Samba Sowe's.

She knelt and thanked God he was alive and still craving for her. She read the letter several times before holding it tight to her bosom singing praises to God and love. She wasted no time in requesting a two weeks leave from her teaching job to travel to the Health Centre to prove her being alive and well but life was a void without him.

She hoped he would love her as much as stated in the letter upon seeing her as she is in the flesh. Time and age had caught up with her but her love remains fresh and yearning for him.

Sure enough after fourteen hours of dusty bumpy roads her transport came to squeaking stop near a big entrance gate and the driver announced, "We have reached Ker Ndumbein Health Centre. I thank all who used my van to travel to this village.

The doctor, Samba Jallow is very generous and able man." Kumba Jallow traveled light with only one small suitcase. She alighted and headed straight to the main building among many white buildings full of people. A young lady who enquired who she wanted to see met Kumba at the office door.

She told Kumba there was a queue that all wanting to see Dispenser Samba lined up and that she should go back to line and fit in before she misses the shaded area. Kumba in her eagerness said, "Darling, I am not a patient but have an urgent need to speak with Samba Sowe for some news from home.

Go in and hand this note to him." She scribbled, "I am finally at your doorsteps but refused entrance. Could you please come out to meet Kumba Jallow, your high school flame?" The young lady took the note to Samba making it the most brilliant day of his life.

He kissed the note and told his assistant to carry on while he sorts out the lady with an urgent message for him. Inside Kumba Jallow, her adrenaline rushed amidst turmoil of desire. She was about to discover that there is nothing riskier than decisions of the heart or more essential than the bond between her and Samba. Her heart rate accelerated upon her seeing Samba Sowe.

He rushed out and landed into the open hands of Kumba Jallow. They embraced and kissed fervently before all present and to the cheers of onlookers. No one ever saw Samba Sowe that romantic or cheerful. They guessed that she might be his lover or wife at the door.

The two kept looking at each as if a miracle got them together once more in this life. Samba Sowe said, "Darling, I have been searching all my life for you until the day that pupil whose grandpa I was treating accidentally mentioned his teacher's name to be Kumba Jallow from Ker Ndumbein.

It rang a bell and I drafted a note placed it in an envelope and prayed it was you. Thank God we are at last in each other's arms. This time I will keep you for good. I will do everything possible to keep you by my side till death." Kumba replied, "Time has stolen our lives but not our hearts. Mine is as green and craving for you as ever. I am yours till death."

The lovebirds held hands walked into the clinic and were welcomed with rapturous applause from the staff and patients alike. Samba Sowe asked the next senior dispenser to carry on seeing the patients for another two hours to allow him arranged a place for his lady guest. The lovebirds took off by the back door to his quarters a couple of hundred yards away from the clinic.

There they ruminated on how worried they were for not linking or having any leads for almost twenty-three years. He fixed tea and food for her and returned to his work humming merrily. His day has been made and no doubts his life was restored by her appearance.

Now it was time for tradition to roll in and allow them marry. Distance would no longer be hindrance. He drafted a note to the district commissioner requesting a month's holiday to go with Kumba Jallow and arrange for their union. This was approved and he and Kumba headed for Ker Nubmen.

At Ndumben Samba Jallow sent a negotiating delegate to bewildered parents of Kumba Jallow. They just could not believe the appearance of the two images before them. They had given up on Samba Sowe ever asking the hand of Kumba Jallow for marriage and today they were before them asking them ratify just that possibility.

Kumba's father, Momadou Jallow, her uncles and even extended families joined in welcoming Samba Sowe and the good news about their daughter. The dowry and all requested were paid instantly and the grand priest came in the next day to sanctify the marriage between Samba and Kumba Jallow.

That done Kumba had to rush back to her school for the wedding ceremony was slated to take place in two or three month's time. Samba and peers set to make the union a very up-bit one for Ker Ndumben.

Soon they were able to buy five three year old bulls, twenty sheep, sixty-eight goats, two hundred bags of rice, millet, and three two hundred liter drum of oil for cooking and the Fulas contributed barrels of fresh milk to go with it on the day of their wedding ceremony.

This done Samba went back to his Health Centre to brief his colleagues who were not only delighted but had their own celebration preparation for the newly wed. This was spear headed by the Commissioner and all nearby the villages. Samba was let off until after his wedding as it requires a bit of preparation.

Nonetheless Samba remained at work until a month to the day of the ceremony before setting for Ker Ndumben to finally take his bride. Mean while shriveling Kumba Jallow gained remarkable weight in those brief months after seeing her love and being guaranteed his heart.

She became more cheerful and congenial than any ever noticed about her. The powerful embers of love had its way in her heart and she was now more eager for the wedding ceremony and having Samba's babies than anything in her life.

The school staff and pupils vowed not to be out done in marking her wedding ceremony. Hence they had her agree to return with her husband for them to show their appreciation for the good mentor she was to them. It was not certain whether she would be transferred to Ker Ndumben secondary school.

Two months later they announced the date of their wedding ceremony to be held at the grand mosques at Ker Ndumben. The venue was chosen for numbers expected attend would not fit in their small three hundred year old nearby small mosque.

Hence the huge ornate grand mosque was apt for the occasion and grandeur to marking of Kumba Jallow and Samba Sowe's wedding. By noon of the wedding day the above massive opulent Mosque's hall, seating more than 3000 was full to capacity.

Marriage between two very popular icons drew almost a quarter of Ker Ndumben and surrounding hamlets into attendance of the ceremony. Those who could not enter the mosque lined the route just to have glance and to wave at the newlywed and to remember heir's some months ago or years gone by. Also hundreds of VIPs drove through to attend the ceremony.

This scenery befits the English royal wedding and reminded the older spectators of Princess Diana's wedding to Princes Charles of England. The hymnals, singing, praises and clapping black style could be heard miles away and throngs in the swayed and or danced while singing their hearts out with pleasure.

When all in the mosque were seated, priest, well attired Samba Sowe and a friend with the wedding ring besides him the priest ushered in the wedding match or tune for Old-man Musa Jallow and Kumba Jallow to be present and for Kumba to take her marriage vows in the presence of God and community.

On arrival old man Musa kissed Kumba Jallow and stepped aside for the ceremony to start. One could not fail to notice the joy and wide-brim smile on Kumba's face on her final of spinsterhood and the taking of a new and would be most rewarding marriage for her and Samba Sowe.

She had been praying for this day and it meant more as it found her a much matured woman, and having had time to compare the pros and cons. This is hers and Samba Sowe portraying love itched in their hearts. Everything about him gives her immense pleasure she could live with. Alas! She was happy to take her vows and done Samba's wedding ring till death do they part.

My dear reader now arrives the moment of truth when the priest offered prayers and then asked if there be any in the congregation who could give reason why the two before them should not be wedded couple.

He urged him or her speaks out or forever holds their peace to allow proceedings of the wedding. None came forth and so Samba Sowe and Kumba Jallow took their vows amidst broad smiles and endless kisses upon being told by the priest that they can kiss.

The people applauded and sang praises to God and to the couple for this joyful and lovely day for the now newly wedded. With the veil removed, Kumba Jallow, now Mrs. Samba Sowe, looked ravishingly beautiful and her wedding dress remains talk of the town for many, many moons.

The motor cade to wedding reception hall was jammed with flowers and presents from on lookers. The flowered hall down town was spectacular and people thronged as before to see the couple. Flowers, rice and greeting cards were thrown at them as they slowly drove through throngs of well-wishers and friends in Ker Ndumbein.

Long speeches were made by numerous of the wedded and people shared delicious cake from the four feet tall wedding cake specially prepared by Flint's best wedding caterers. At the end the couple flew to Edinburgh in England to have their honeymoon in private at one of the many castles in that city.

Very few weddings matched the popularity of this ker Ndumben's couple. They returned three weeks later to their various occupations much happier and ready for the jobs than ever before. The real wedding took place at Ker Ndumbein where nearly five thousand villagers attended the ceremony and festivities that followed. The Mayor, Borum Deka, of Ker Ndumbe gave special recognition of the union by proclamation that it be yearly set as public holiday in remembrance of joy the two brought to the village. Attendants gorged themselves to almost choking levels and dance right through two days of festivities.Kumba's school pupil threw in a fare well dance for her as she secured a transfer to Ker Ndumben High School so that she could near husband Samba Sowe who manned the Health Centre at the place. The fairy tale of craving love yielded numerous twins between Kumba and Samba who are still married and in their late sixties.

Nothing is greater than love

You Are Heaven on Earth

Nothing is more soothing than having met the perfect gentleman or lady as a mate. It turns this life into heaven and one clamoring to savor every minute of life's joy. Money though able to get us comfort never can buy love. It surely feels like being in heaven when love is at its height.

Nengbali kinte and Lang Karajang are our lucky match and we will see how enamored they got through this romantic fairy tale that dwarfs Alice in wonderland story. Neither came from chieftaincies or abodes of kings and queens.

However they had something they would never exchange with a golden crown or house full of diamonds. Yes, their love was unique and endearing to them. It made life worth living as well as enduring. They were the epitaph and zenith of pleasure in each other's presence.

They wrote poems and sang numerous love songs to each other. Their hearts were so engraved that neither of them would eat in the absence of the other. Except being conjoin twins they were one in thought and deed.

They daily shower each other with presents and encouragements. Nengbali crossed path with Lang Karajang in 1956 at the "Mansa Bengo," village thanks giving festival held at Njakunda in Lower Badibou, the Gambia. It was love at first sight for both of them. However, it was Lang Karajan who pried the Pandora's' box open, as most village girls feel uncomfortable being pushy towards males.

They are not your common pussy riot one may come across in other regions. It's tabooed and eventually results in lack of respect for the flirting girl. No bimbo is respected in village settings. From that hour of their sighting each other onto to the end of the festivities these two had no recollection of the dynamism or activity that transpired.

They were deeply involved with each other than the ongoing thanks giving festivities. Lang introduced himself after a brief trance saying, "I am Lang Karajang but my friends delight in calling me Lang. You are so beautiful. What is your name?

They call me Nengbali Kinte. I am pleased to make your acquaintance. I hope this would not be our last meeting? I am from Kinte Kunda Janneya. And you?" Lang said, "I am from Kinte Kunda Marong Kunda a stone throw from your village. How come our path never crossed until today? Are you spoken for or married?

I like an honest answer because only that cements hearts together for eternity. By the way I teach at Salikenye Primary School. I would be deeply delighted by your visiting me at the school." Nengbali smiled while pretending to be shy at the same time. At the end she said, "I am an honest person who hates deception which nowadays seem trend in most men.

Yes, I have strong feelings for you and have no doubts it could nurture to a most worthy end for both of us. No, I am neither spoken for nor am I married yet. It would be wise of you to act soon.

As for visiting you it would at this juncture be frowned upon and for me that is too soon a cause to take. Tell me more about you other than your teaching carrier. Do you have a girl friend or been spoken for back at Kinte Kunda Marong Kunda? Will your family ratify our union? Tell no lies please."

Lang Kanjura paused in reflection for a brief moment and assured Nengbali that he did had a girl friend while at the Teacher Training College but it fizzled out for the better and the concerned was now happily married to her Armitage high school class mate.

In addition he said, 'I love you dearly and have no doubts my family will welcome you with kindness and love you never had in your life. I assure you that I will stand by you and our children throughout my earthly life. Also, I will from hence forth never let you out of my sight." This left Nengbali partially reassured there remains some distance between their locations.

Would he run into another beauty before the end of the day, next week or months after? Was it infatuation or real? She was not going let her fears derail her from gaining confidence love of man she would give her heart at any reasonable cost or price.

Both having come out clean they held hands and walked to a more quitter place to plan the next traditional moves to accelerate their union. At which place they broke the first tribal taboo that is never kiss on the first date or on meeting the first time for one never know the end result.

The lovebirds ironed out more doubts and talked about how to bring up their children and what university they should attend. Yes this was back in the sixties, few years after our gaining independence from Britain.

Ambition was riff amongst villagers, as they too want to catch up with those in the capital who literally run the affairs of state because of their educational backgrounds or skills thereof. They too want to participate in our evolution and as well share the national cake.

There was a Jeweler's shop twenty-five minutes away where the two went before rejoining the ceremony afoot. They at first widow shopped before the lovebirds finally stopped at a local Jeweler stall and Lang Kanjura asked Nengbali Kinte to close her eyes.

He picked the most pristine and decorated necklace had it wrapped and then they continued to a flower stand. Here he selected freshly picked red rose and Bougainvilleas and with the wrapped gift handed it to Nengbali Kinte saying, "It is for our pleasure and my love for you."

Again tears of joy rolled down lovely cheeks of Nengbali Kinte as she opened the wrapping. She said, "I love you but are you a magician? This was the first necklace that caught my fancy when we were at the Jeweler's stall. Thank you very much I shall have it around my neck with you and when you are away on honest business."

Soon the people started dispersing signaling time for the lovebirds to rejoin before being prematurely exposed. They left very happy for having such a marvelous romantic encounter. Nengbali threw an air kiss towards Lang and said just leave your lips planted on mine until we reach home.

I am in heaven with you being on my side." The festivities came to close four days later and it was time to say goodbye but no goodbyes as the two decided to travel to

Kinte Kunda for Lang Karajeng's family to meet those of Nembail Kinte to ask for her hand in marriage. At first Nembali's uncles put up resistance to the approaching on grounds that Lang Karajang was not well paid as junior teach and that their sibling deserves a better future that a may be or likely upgrading.

Nembali along with her mum got furious about the money grabbing deal her Uncles were from Lang Karajang seeking indirectly. Hence Nengbali boldly stepped forward and said, "I would like to go on record that any filibuster to the union will lead me to elope with him and we will go far away to another country were we would spend the rest of our lives together without you."

The threat was taken seriously for the family knows that this girl never changes her mind once she decides to act. So the uncles backed down immediate allowing amicable discussions and negotiations for the dowry and all other mandinka tradition that would allow the two to be wedded in due course.

It took three days for everything to be ironed out and to the surprise of the uncles Lang's entourage deposited three times more than was asked for in addition to lucrative presents of diamond studded gold necklaces, bangles and expensive shoes from both England and Italy they brought for Nembali Kinte.

This show of love and strength from Lang Karajang pulled the rug underneath critics and made their engagement the talk of several villagers for years to follow. It left Nembali Kinte very proud of Lang Karajang and loved him more than she ever thought she could have for another human besides her parents.

On completion of the first roll of the traditional ball Lang dashed back to his school to teach, as there was an agreed gap of three months before the real wedding ceremony takes place. Nengbali Kinte visited him briefly at the school before returning to Kinte Kunda Janneya, her home the same day.

During their time there were no telephones, televisions, cinemas or Internet Cafes to wild time. Villagers had lived life without these modern delusional gadgets.Both parents worked together to proper prepare for the wedding festivities and catering of attendants normally use this lull period.

From Lang's side a hundred goats, twenty bulls, 70 sheep, 100 bags of rice, ten drums of cooking oil, and a heap of vegetables of all kinds. On the day of the ceremony the fishermen vowed to provide four canoes of good catch as contribution for people's consumption by the coming attendance. My friend love is indeed powerful and can pull great effort together in no time.

Lang was given leave to enable him attend his wedding a month before the actual chosen date of the ceremony. The grand finale came ushered in with clear blue skies accompanied by cool breeze.

The bride and bridegroom were immaculate, smashing to behold in their traditional dress that most girls wished their day turns out half as impressive as the one they are joyously living through. Poets and scribes wrote and sang history of two families from time immemorial.

The music and dancing crescendo could be heard many miles away and the village was innovated. At the end Lang Karajang with now Mrs. Nengbali Karajang besides him thanked the people thus, "Fellow farmers, Nengbali and I are overwhelmed by your kindness, wordiness and indeed for joining us to make this the most unique life experience Mrs. Nembali Karajang and I.

We love you and are grateful for the communal show. Thank you for being custodians of tradition, which we should never loose. God bless and good-bye." He then turned towards Nengbali, kissed her and said, "You are my heaven on earth!" The newlyweds lived happily forever and are now fifty years in marriage rewarded with doctors and lawyer off springs serving the community.

FK, THE SOUL OF MY HEART

Love in full bloom

Love on the Blue Seases

It is said that at sea one has to have steady feet but falling in love under such momentous magnificence we are to discover bugles the mind. Imagine being on board the world's largest luxury cruiser queen Mary 11 along with 3600 other passengers and being chaperoned round luxuriant amnesties befitting only royalty.

The tour starts at the planetarium and art gallery and when one reaches what is referred to as the H2O Zone or spray ground one is mesmerized with colorful fiberglass sculpture shooting jets of water, geysers shooting from the ground and water cannons. Here a lazy river and waterfall draws spectacular attention.

At night the area transforms into integration of an incredible lighting system that change into a sculptured garden.Nothing comes close to the H2O Zone's sport pool located in the main pool area. One of the pools is used for games, ranging from baseball and volleyball to synchronized swimming with designated lanes for lap swimming.

One can relax at the second pool or watch the night sea transformed into open-air nightclub with a large dance floor between the two pools. The chaperone takes us to a 445-foot shopping arcade, dining and entertainment boulevard that spans the length of an entire football field. At night, a promenade hosting street parades, put on by staff, commencing from a revolutionary new descending bridge amidst a fanfare of music, lasers and light.

We are told guests can also relax reading at the 3600 Book Nook. They can also find fame at the On Air Club, karakas venues with state of the arts theatrical lighting, video cameras, flat screen TV and even "green screen". Aspiring music stars, we are told, can record their own music video. Shows are viewed at the Art Deco style Arcadia Theatre that normally features three classic shows per night. It was at such a onetime experience in life that Dr. Seni Sanneh and Dr. Kunsa Marong met by the poolside.

Both are medical doctors and hence they decided to visit the Book Nook and browse among the impressive 3600 books. For some reason Dr. Seni Sanneh was reading Romeo and Juliet when she was interrupted by the presence of a good-looking gentleman who was trying to get her attention.

At first she paid no attention but moved to a more quitter section leaving a seat vacant by her side. Dr. Marong seized the opportunity and sat on the vacant chair next to Dr. Seni Sanneh. She kept her cool but once on a while their gaze met and then they would pretend to fixate upon a nearby statute.

The embers of love got restless in their bosoms. However it was Dr. Marong who finally plucked up enough courage to bell the cat saying, "Hello beautiful. You have fascinated me since setting eyes on you. I am Dr. Kunsa Marong from Marong Kunda in the Gambia. What is your lovely name?"

A girlish shyness overtook our thirty-five year old Dr. Seni Sanneh. She almost with eyes reverted or looking at the floor replied' "What a small world. I am also Gambian from Brufut in the Kombos, Western Division to be exact. My name is Dr. Seni Sanneh but you can from now on just call me Dr. Sanneh.

I am the new consultant slated to take over the Royal Victoria Hospital's (RVH) pediatric wards in Banjul.

Hence I am trying to have the most rest before starting the challenge. Where do you work and what is your specialty in Banjul?" Both laid their books down and carried on a conversation that would cement them forever.

Dr. Marong said, "I am a thoracic surgeon and head of the department of surgery at the RVH. I am on leave and In case it interests you I am single and I just believe I have met my soul mate on board the Queen Mary 11." This drew a broad smile of approval from Dr Sanneh who asked, "How do you know I would be interested in you? He replied, "My love and gut feelings are never far from being 99.9% right all the time.

And I dare tell you I love you Dr. Sanneh."The candor and suddenness of developed love was overwhelming. Hence Dr. Sanneh went into damage modification and drive. She asked, "How much do you know about me and what made you so brave to propose at the spore of the moment?

Could it be that you are being infatuated with me? If so such links come to a sad and abrupt end which I do not intend to experience."Dr. Maron interjected by letting her know love is timeless and blind and only the heart can tell whom it likes. He added, "I am certain of my feelings for you but you do have all right to reject me as long as you are not punishing me for a hurt another caused you.

I am certain of the feeling that this discovery could change everything as there is romance in the air in the new person to be in my life." Dr. Sanneh, who was more enamored than she displayed calmed her colleague saying, "Fear not. I was just checking the dept and commitment of your involvement with me. Too many times men tell women they adore them only because they just want to have a one-time affair and disappear thereafter." The ship rocked hard and they fell into each other's arms kissing spontaneously.

It took another ten minutes of ceaseless kissing and mumbling before the two came to the natty gritty of the day. Now relaxed Dr. Sanneh asked if Dr. Marong was spoken for or does he have an incomparable fiancé. She insisted on the truth coming out saying' "We must from now on be frank to see which direction this warmth will take.

I love you but I do not rush anything about me. I do need to let you know I will text a friend to find out about your social history in Banjul. Do you drink or smoke? I cannot stand drunks or the smell of tobacco in my bedroom. All I want to smell is my husband not some poison."

Dr. Marong got excited about the direction things are taking. He said, "Rest assured that none of my relatives selected a wife for me and I have no fiancé in Banjul or the Americas. I was too busy to become a surgeon serving the Gambia.

The thought of marrying ran into my mind during this relax holiday moment but never did I contemplate on any one until my seeing you three hours ago at the shopping area. I followed you to where we are now because I will never, left to me alone, leave you alone for the rest of my life."

The two held hands never stopping to look into the other's eyes while pouring their hearts out. In the end they agreed to give three weeks or a month's wait before Dr. Marong sends his envoys to ask for her hand in marriage.

The reason given was that she needed more time to reflect upon and to have feeling of life in big city Banjul before tying herself into a difficult situation. From now on they will follow tradition. Even as doctors they will not go beyond kissing and hugging until their honeymoon day. They spent the rest of the evening seated close together watching movies at the Arcadia Theatre.

They agreed to attend entertainment activities at the art Deco Style the following day. After the show Dr. Marong walked his soul mate up to the door of her cabin and bid her sweet dreams and told her that they should meet for breakfast at the main dining hall.

They kissed and separated with the surgeon dancing his way to his bunker. Soon Dr. Sanneh heard from her friend Kujeja Sarr about enquiries she asked her carry out about Dr. Marong. So far Kujeja said, "All I could come up with is that he has no ties but many women find him very attractive however because of his aloofness and never paying attention to their flirting they believe him impotent.

He is uncharted waters that comes from a good and respected family and would be trophy worth to fight for." The two ladies laughed at the ensuing battle because Dr. Marong is now fully committed to this handsome and talented surgeon.

She was not going to let a fly land on him or take him away from her without a fierce battle. He belongs to her. They spoke over many things until the other's card ran out. As for Dr. Marong, he took a war shower, entered the days' development in diary and went straight to bed sleeping like log till the next day when the maid came to refresh his bed.

This is an everlasting bond of love

He ran to the shower and took a quick bath and sure enough Dr. Sanneh was at one of tables reading the menu hoping to see him soon. He kissed her and said "Good morning darling. I am sorry for being late. It has never been a habit to be late but I slept like a log after our parting being certain that we are one from now on."

He then took his seat facing her while she throws smiles that beams showing pearly white ivory teeth that made Dr. Marong feeling lucky to have her as a wife.

They spoon-fed each other at breakfast and then later walked hand in hand to the Jeweler's shop where Dr. Marong bought her a very high quality diamond engagement ring. He placed it on her ring finger and said "From now on I am yours for good or for bad, in thick or thin as we ply through life."

Dr. Sanneh with misty eyes but joyous heart let a few teardrops down her cheek as she looked up and said, "I love you even if you turn a leper. I love you and I will proudly wear it for the rest of our lives." They ended at the swimming pool and swarm for an hour before retiring on the deck watching dolphins and sharks swim by the huge luxury cruiser.

Later they had their dinner together and went to watch professional entertainers and celebrity make their night before retiring to bed. Soon the Cruiser anchored at Port Prince in Haiti where the future couple boarded a plane, again seated next to each other and headed for the Gambia, West Africa.

The Boeing GA 737 landed smoothly after ten hours flight at the Yundum International tarmac with both eager to rejoin family and friends. The Director of Health who after the airport formalities drove them to Banjul in his black official limo met them at the VIP lounge.

They were pleased to be at the smiling coast of Africa and for Dr. Sanneh this would be her second visit in three years. She was inundated and busies familiarizing with younger generation of the family. The next day she took a quick trip to Brufut, her home village to join her ninety-year-old mother.

She spent a forth night there and returned to Banjul after revealing her intent to be wedded to Dr. Marong head of surgery at the RVH. Her mother blessed her and looked forward to attending ceremony.

Dr. Marong had similar ground breaking move, which was to be kept under wrap until a month after as agreed by him and Dr. Seni Sanneh. Both resumed work at the RVH with Dr. Sanneh busy reorganizing the Pediatric department for better service and record keeping of childhood diseases brought to her unit.

Dr. Marong was up to his neck with surgical cases to be done and routine of the day hardly allowed him see Dr. Sanneh who was ways on the other side of the main hospital. There are hardly lunch breaks in place like the RVH. The workload only allows a short time for one to have bite of pancake with a cup of Ataya or tea before resuming job.

It will not be until 5:00 pm before the lovebirds could meet briefly to arrange the next social day's agenda for them. It being Saturday, they decided to have a sumptuous dinner at hotel Teranga and later attend Yusu Ndurrs' Mballah show scheduled to start at 10:30 pm at the same hotel.

Both doctors are great fans of Yusu Ndurr and they never missed his performances. The evening went well for them and both met lot of friends in attendance. With the show over and managing to secure Yusu Ndurr's signed autograph the fiancés drove home elated about their choice of each other.

At Dr. Marong's home they kissed and bid each other sweet dreams and to see at the staff meeting set for 11:00 am CEO's office the next day. Heads turned toward our thirty five year old now head of Pediatrics, moments after making her entrance to the hall.

Some doctors were not able to stop whistling in appreciation of her elegance and petrifying beauty. Dr. Sanneh walked straight to where Dr. Marong was seated and planted herself next to him. This she did to signal her interest in him and no other male in the room.

CEO Dr. Mariama Jongfolo who chaired the meeting jokingly said "Dr. Sanneh, grant it you will cause lot of fluttering hearts if not fibrillation in some present hearts. Welcome to the RVH.

We always are pleased to have citizens manning the affairs of our departments. You have my full support and backing for any change you may deem needed for better service to our children. Again we are happy to welcome you aboard RVH." Dr. Sanneh beamed setting the men wanting to kiss her and said, "Thank you Dr. Jongfolo, I assure all I will do my best for our people and will always be a team member where the staff is concerned.

I am happy to be home amongst able Gambian colleagues."

Dr. Mariama Jongfolo read out matters to be catered and asked if any had new ideas on how to improve service at the RVH. Dr. Musa Camara, always a show off started saying, "We need instill discipline in the wards for most of the younger nurses are about getting out of hand in manner they talk back to doctors and their seniors."

The CEO promised to talk to the Matron about his observations. Dr. Camara is one of those who have habit of trying to impress new staff at such meetings but this one eluded him for she never once looked at him. He noticed and was not going to end things at that.

Hence right after the meeting he elbowed his way to almost positioning himself between Drs. Sanneh and Marong. Dr. Sanneh wasted no time in putting him in his proper place. She told him to have courtesy, as they really do not need him around their private discusions.

So he walked away in shame and never spoke to Dr. Sanneh for a long time. He just had crush for her and did not know how to approach Dr. Sanneh.Drs. Marong and Sanneh laughed at Dr. Camara's boyish behavior the next time they were together.

Dr. Marong assured her that, "I fear nothing because of believe that you are a decent lady in love with one you choused. Try to keep Dr. Camara away from me before he creates more trouble for me."

Dr. Sanneh told him that she would keep her distance and would only allow professional conduct between her any other man, especially Dr. Camara. The two lady doctors, Drs. Sanneh and Jongfolo, gelled and met several times to chat or even discourses the men working with them.

Never did two women agree than these veteran doctors of the RVH. Now that the first huddle of competition was taken care off Dr. Marong's uncle and company met the Sanneh Family at Brufut to ask for Dr. Seni Sanneh's hand in marriage to Dr. Kunsa Marong.

The formalities and eventual sanctioning of marriage between Dr. Seni Sanneh and Dr. Kunsa Marong was foregone conclusion. Every aspect went smoothly and the high priest at the grand mosque sanctioned the union of these medical lovebirds.

The wedding ceremony was a big bash and everyone loved and enjoyed the occasion well. The music and local dancing went on for days before celebrants finally call it quit. Unlike most newlyweds who run to Europe for their honeymoon experience; the couple spent their honeymoon at hotel Sope in Dakar, Republic of Senegal. They returned to their posts two weeks after and the Royal Victoria Hospital reciprocated by throwing its own wedding ceremony for the two newlywed doctors. The two thousand-sitter hall at the RVH was full to capacity and again, music, dancing; praises and well-wishers took the show.

Dr. Seni Sanneh took the opportunity to thank the staff and friends for making her day memorable. She said, "Comrades, thank you for sharing our joy and for letting us know we have friends in you." And jokingly added, "Ladies, what are you waiting?

Grab the boys before someone else beat you to your dream love. Dr. Marong and I were meant for each other and he is the only real love for me. Thanks a million to all of you." This fairy tale union emanating from incidental meeting on board the world's largest luxury cruiser was fantasy by itself. The couple practiced medicine and raised plenty children and have just celebrated their 50th wedding anniversary.

Love is in this smile. She found her friend at Njawara

Tall, Angelic and Handsome

Tall and dark was not the only grand qualities nature bequeathed the man whose romantic life we are about to unveil. Abdoulie Fatajo was just at the end of his manuscript acknowledging help given by friends and his agent reassuring them that without them he could not have done it.

And to his family he conveys all his love, and also offering a big thanks to his wife and children. He said, "Without you I would never be strong to do the job. Thank you for everything. But more so for the twenty glorious years of happiness, you and the children you gave me."It was at this juncture that a knock came faintly through the front door.

He hesitated as to who could be visiting at such late hours of the night. He asked, "Could it be burglars or some homeless seeking shelter and food?" To be on the safe side he sneaked to the upper floor and gingerly slides the window to have a good look at what was anxiously wrapping his door.

To his greatest surprise the figure looked very much like that of his long time girl friend but now a grown lady. He rushed to the door and asked, "Is that who I thought it could be?" A shy but very clear female voice said, "Abdoulie, what is the matter with you? Open the door. It is Mariama Jallow.

Do not pretend to have forgotten me." He nervously opened the door to let her in but hoping that it was no serious thing that brought her to his abode at such a late hour. He said, "Come through and welcome to my modest home. Sorry about the mess. He conducted a quick tour of his modest rooms, which were each well decorated, according to Mariama, to a princely standard. There was an enormous kitchen gleaming with stainless steel and clean environs.

Mariama's big eyes and slim body swirled his head. She was stunningly beautiful and would sway men on the first sight. Her smile was pure and ravishing in addition to her sexy looks. She stood in front of Abdoulie like a phoenix. He took Mariama on a tour of the rooms and finally said, "This is my humble bedroom.

A split second later they both were scrumptiously enquiring each other while recalling old memories at the same time searching for hidden signs that one fancies about others. Mariama noticed that a stereo was stationed at the far end of the seating place with stacks of CDs besides it was a fifty inch television in the medium size room.

Next to the telephone were stacks of books and a few glossies and local cartoons of Zumorimaro, Spicer and suleran and more magazines littering the floor. Abdoulie was embarrassed by it but Marriama told him not to worry about it he like most modern men would rather be with pumped up dolls or gaze at glossies or fantasies like that on the floor than real hot flesh.

The remark was not funny but he took it with gusto on the chin. However, they ended up in the bedroom and with the rain pouring mad outside, inside there was a romantic storm about to brew between this long time lovers. Soon Abdoulie Fatajo began to kiss her passionately on her lips; his hands drifting unconsciously under her top with the silence only punctuated by their deep breathing which became heavier with every extra heartbeat. He had missed her since their last high school encounter behind the teacher's desk. Now she was like an uncharted map whose points he most connects to the feminine point. Hence his hand continued exploring further by dropping into her knickers while his fingers teased between her legs setting them apart.

The rain poured harder and soon the two lovers were naked in bed. He rolled over, lay on top of her and again kissed her passionately on the lips, neck and you know where to touch while saying, "Believe me you are so gorgeous and a turn on."

She relented and pushed her legs wide apart to let him in to have a vigorous sex in compensating lost time. She savored every minute of it. She afterwards lay with a huge smile stuck on her face. Never in her dreams did she ever experience such great and fantastic sexual encounter.

She was not going to wait long to have another go at it, again and again as if one time of this fabulous lovemaking was not enough. His leg was pressed tightly against her and his hands never stopped searching and reaching for her buttocks.

They were itching for sex and would not peel apart because of continuous need by our lovebirds. She told Fatim, her best friend, "Never in my wildest dreams did I think that sex could feel as stupendous as Abdoulie Fatajo gave and made me feel the last time. He brought the woman in me out and lovingly too.

I must have been born stupid to let him tarry away for as long as has happened. He gave me several orgasms while maintaining a hard-on. He was adept at hitting my buttons the first time for he knew exactly what to do and with which part of the body to arise. I bet you my life he will never escape again." Fatim chuckled and added, "Most girls yearn to be his. Hence you most work hard to persevere." The next day brought the sad news of the passing of Mariama's dad and she had to retreat fast to her village to attend the funeral service some fifty miles away. Abdoulie joined her at the funeral service but had to return right after.

This was not a good omen for Mariama. Abdoulie was too good to leave alone but social taboos forbid Mariama leaving until after the forty nights after the passing of her father. Meanwhile Abdoulie, like most celebrates and being so handsome could not wrest himself from ladies. He was their man who they will never give respite at any time.

He was hot topic in the rice fields and at the market and where ever young women gathered. Mariama's fears soon materialized. Kumba Taskati-Seyi had an eye on our handsome Abdoulie and had made up her mind to confront him with her love for him.

She told a confidant, "I met a deliciously gorgeous man I believe we are in love. There was a connection I felt for this man that I have never experienced. It was like electricity flowing all through my torso. I will fight tooth and nail to win him. He is my heart and sunshine."

Mrs. Fatou Koma-Ceesay

One hindrance for Kumba was advanced age and Kumba was, in local terms, being one of the richest business ladies with connection at high levels of politics. She was ready to use both achievements to her advantage in wooing her heart's desire.

Hence, she let word reach Abdoulie that she has an urgent need to talk business with him at hotels Teranga that 6:00 pm prompt. She even sent one of her limos to pick him up at 5:45 pm. Abdoulie, being certain of efficacy of his good assets, complied and attended the rendezvoused as stipulated.

Gorgeous Waitress served them at the table of her choice far away from listening ears. She started the inquisition by asking him if he had girl friends or was he spoken for, meaning arranged marriage, by relative. He assured her that none of the questions really applied to him.

He is a free man forging for a bright and prosperous future for him and his future family. She then asked, "Do you see yourself loving women of my caliber and age? Or if I were to let you know that I had serious crush on you. How would you respond to that?"

Abdoulie placed his head between his hands, bowed and after thinking for a long five minutes, which seemed an eternity to Kumba, raised his head and looked directly into her face and said, "Madam, love is blind and does go to the deserving one.

I am on the other hand not for sale nor would I have a partner who only wish to use me as a showcase to tell young ladies that even though she is old she still can snatch good looking fellows right under their very noses. Your wealth does not move an inch of me nor your promise of holidaying on golden yachts and partying in lavish hotel suites or providing special made designer clothes. I had suspected your motive for tonight's meeting but am not one that beats about the bush. I do not love you and cannot see myself changing that stance. There are young ladies out there that I am enamored to but not you. Money does not buy true love for love is priceless. It belongs to the heart.

Thank you for a lovely evening and please do not cross my path or that of Mariama Jallow. She is a decent woman my heart cherishes dearly." In shock Kumba Taskati-sey could only apologize for trying for she too loved this hunk of a man.

To show her sincerity she let him ride back home in the limo that collected him earlier on in the day. Now news reached poor mourning Mariama before Abdoulie's message reached her. It made Mariama furious that the man she loved would dump her in the midst of her mourning period. She drafted a quick but tearful note to Abdoulie. It read in part thus:

Dear love,

Some sad news just reached me today. It is rumored that rich lady Kumba Taskati-sey has been trying to buy you out for her false prestige. Please let me continue believing that you are neither a flag nor one that sell his dignity for gilders.

Remember, all that glitters is not gold. She may be rich and wielding such prowess to be able to purchase young males at wimp. That is no love nor is it true love that you and I had for each other since our teenage days. Again, I am restless in addition to losing my dad I do not want to lose you to some one that does not love you but dying to align with your handsomeness.

Again, I have no love other yours and look forward to our union soon. For the love of my life you are permanently etched in me anytime and with me everywhere. Please write or send friends to clarify your position in this deadly story. Never let me go or death will lay its chilly hands over me for good. Forever etched in my heart
 Love & kisses
 Mariama Jallow-Fatajo
On receiving this letter Abdoulie Fatajo wasted no time to get himself on his bike and dash to Mariama's home village brought in the know about my heart's true yearning for him until it was too late. His perfect body and good looks lends a smash hit with ladies.

I see myself entrenched and completely intertwine with his life. I dream daily being wrapped by his strong manly arms.My finding out that he was a man with more marbles and morals made me even love him more and I will die respecting and loving him.

He is an honest, thrust worthy and rare man indeed. I know because I have dealt with all sorts of men but none come close to dignity this man has and respect he has for women. I wish most men were like him in thought."
Legend has it that Mariama and Kumba Taskati-sey became the best of friends to a point it was Mariama Fatajo who suggested Abdoulie Fatajo to have Kumba Taskati-sey as a second wife.

This he did and both ladies had lovely children for him and held him as their sunshine and with great esteem and love they never experienced until he came into their lives. Again, all is well that ends well. Love never stops intriguing the mind. None ever foresaw that Kumba Taskati-sey would ever be married but love knows better.

Abdoulie's refusal to betray Mariama had landed him bonanza, as he became a very rich man that had respect of his community and region. This marriage was akin to that of Alice in wonderland tales of princes picking the coveted sandals left behind Even though tradition does not allow it Mariama had to sneak out at the dead of night and meet with her lover at a friend's house located at the outskirts of the village.

The two lovebirds in brief but very warm way renewed their commitments to each other and Abdoulie promised to start the ball rolling for them to tie the knot and finally rest any doubts to their being husband and wife. Abdoulie was tired of multi-millionaire women who are only after his good looks and sexual prowess.

He felt insulted by such motives and refuses to be treated like a beauty sex object. He was fully aware that beauty like flower petals do fade with time. So is the superficial relationship money offers. There is no monetary price for his heart or to put it bluntly his love.

He wants pure love from the heart as demonstrated by Mariama Jallow. He is willing to climb the steep hills and gorges of life with her than be dumped by a rich lady who found herself another pretty commodity. Mariama Jallow joined him right after the family's morning period.

Two weeks after Abdoulie Fatajo sent Kola nuts asking for hand of pretty Mariama Jallow to be his wedded wife. The family agreed and soon they were married in a subdued ceremony as a mark of respect to Mariama's deceased father.

Kumba although was undoubtedly laden hearted contributed a fortune to the wedding and gave the couple a brand new Mercedes Benz as a wedding present.

Asked why she gave this lavishness, she replied, "Because Abdoulie is every woman's dream and I have always loved him but he was not.

Musa Manneh and his younger brother, Uk 2017

Teenage Love

The teenage years are the most difficult for parents likewise the most deceptive for the fledgling adult just on the brink of adulthood and maturity. Parents are over whelmed by their teenager's liveliness, vivacity, and dynamism and above all most parents wonder where these got their ceaseless energies.

They leave parents animated asking where the drive came from. Add love to the above state one gets a much pepped lady indeed. We will with patients indulge our curiosity in the teenage love life of Muminatou Faal and Basiru Njie both at Malpha High School in Banjul.

Miss Muminatou Faal came from Banjul City and Basiru Njie was a native born of Bara village in the North Bank of the River Gambia. The two met at a debating class early 1987 and fell in love. The vigor and enthusiasm with which these kids displayed their affection for each other was very endearingly unique.

They adored each other and would spend hours on the mobile talking. In class Munminatou would write a message and have it passed through some human convoy unbeknown to the teachers. The note may talk about where to meet during break or about something funny she forgot to tell him before assembly.

Basiru was more secretive and would just signal by shrugging his shoulders that he got the note without looking back at her at the back raw. There was always pandemonium at the back row where almost all the beauties of the class choose to stay so they can play game of Jekyll and Hyde on the teachers or their lovers.

Two minutes after the teacher taken a break to chat with the principal hell broke loose. One of the pupils threw a Paperclip; then someone else threw an exercise book. And in another minute, almost everyone was throwing things, standing on chairs or mock fighting under tables. One of the students grinned and said, "There is lot more fund in this than doing mathematic."

What is this life without a teenage life to remember; stars and a beauty's glance and watch how they dance. Do not misread their jokes for these two take their schooling seriously with dedication. They were always either the top scorers or the second highest in all their class tests. Basiru and Muminatou were pride of Malpha High School. Muminatou aspires to become a Pediatrician at the Royal Victoria Hospital in Banjul while Basiru looks forward to becoming, what he refers as, the surgeon general of the Gambia.

Being in the sciences made it easier for them to study together and have a go at each other. Both loved tennis and swimming sports. When Basiru and his mates visit Muminatu the house resembles an engulfing tidal wave of pillow fights, loud music, they play games on the computer, at times climbing on the suffers and running around as if at a football field or some werewolves.

At school they were always voted class prefects and voice of the student organization. Muminatou served as the secretary for the school's newspaper, Malpha News, while Basiru served as its editor. The staff respected them and gave all assistance to encourage them grow into the force they aspire.In their teenage love days there was never sexual encounter as it was frowned upon for children of their age to be indulged by the community.

Proximity at times lore them to it but they both resisted raw electrifying temptation and agreed to wait for their marriage day especially during their honeymoon than dishonoring themselves because of very freaky moments of desire. Munminatu puts it this way, "A part of me confounded by love and fear would almost sign a pact as your accomplice.

It is a tinkering female defect no one can help but hope takes over." Basiru retorted, "Hope perches in the soul and ceaselessly sings melodious soothing tunes without words. My sun sets to arise again with I might be at the gutter but I look up at the star you are seating. You are always a rose in the deeps of my heart."

Both laughed and walked backed hand in hand to safe site of their home. Beneath the brooding wing of happiness the two danced their way home to the envy of angels. They epitomized legacy of youthful love. It goes without doubt that these are brilliant matured minded teenagers who were not going to experiment frivolously. They became icons their peers immolate and pride of their parents, school and community.

Pericles says it best when he said, "What you leave behind is not what is engraved on stone monuments but what is woven into the lives of others." The teenage life enshrined above touched many giving them happiness, at times challenging and at times making the love goddess envious.

They made hearts of the elderly feel young as their acts fill them with love. The Greek proverb puts it thus, "A heart that loves is always young." Love was always on the side of Muminatu Faal and Basiru Njie the pride of Malpha High School.

R-L: Fatou Koma, Famatanding Ceesay, Alagie Ceesay, Binta Ceesay and Roheyata Ceesay

The mystry Bere Kolong queen of love

At a region called Bere Kolong near Chakunda in the Badibous dwelled the most beautiful female figurine that only a few unfortunate young men chance to encounter. She is said to be perched amidst panorama of roses the like of which is found nowhere on earth.

Calamitous indeed for this sweetheart of the spirit chouses her lover and wards off any female that would dare flirt for her chosen mate. Her name was Jina Nyima, Alias Bere Kolong Masibo or the invisible spirit of love in the local vernacular.

By the way Bere Kolong means stone well. Jina Nyima was so tantalizing that any man other than the one she selected, gazing upon her is immediately turned into a stone at the position he stood. Hence up to today there stood many tall stones in the shape of men near Bere Kolong. It is now a tourist sight.

Her method of recruiting a lover starts as early as when the male child was born. It is said that through her supernatural powers she would make her new male partner grow faster than most children, bigger, taller and normally a lot stronger than any of his peers. She infuses these traits to send signal to other humanoid females who might set eyes on her lover.

Inna Musa was Jina nyima's father and he regretted his daughter being in love with humanoids instead of Jini like her. Because of this irreconcilable state between them he cast a curse upon her and varnished to Jina Dou and never returns to Bere Kolong. Jina Nyima lived in a huge cave near the milky well whose waters served her.

Only this milk like water quenches her thirst any other would leave her dehydrated and unable to function. It was reported that only one soothsayer or chief village Witchdoctor at a nearby village knew that the water from this particular source was her life being cursed by her father Jina Musa.

To secure her life she cast a guarding-spirit around the well making humans coming ten meters to it go blind instantly. Any who ventures beyond the ten-meter boundary are turned into stone, hence the name Bere Kolong in the local lingo.

It sounded crewel that such a beauty would guard its jewel fiercely and so close to its heart. This no man's zone enables her to walk free and live free with the man of her heart. In this way, she literally steals her mate and keeps him kidnapped at the cave while feeding him the best kingly feasts and drinks from the heavenly milky waters of Bere Kolong.

In the event of any girl getting astray to the well to fetch water she is normally not turned into stone but her mind is cryptically controlled and she ends up being a servant at the cave. Should this servant chouse to have any feeling for her mate both are instantly blinded and turned into weeds to be fed upon by grazing animals.

Jina Nyima is said to have many half-man and halftime mutants roaming about, especially at night. Villages claim to hear them singing and dancing or just playing magic to entertain themselves. The natives even believed that men with extreme physique amongst them may be her children she planted in the region.

Friday the villagers for fear of angering the jubilant jinni kid accepted Friday nights as self-imposed curfew nights. The young jinni kids' playground was on top of mountain Kuku Konko near the famous Bao Blong creek. Atop of Kuku Konko balls of fireworks could be seen filling the night skies to the periled of any venturing to the sight. If any is seen one is normally surrounded by a powerful cyclone and swept to the cave to serve as slaves doing the chores for her mate.

The mystery Jini does not eats but needs the milky water to enable a human male to inseminate her. It serves as a sedative, which allows the process to take place. She is known to be the only Jini that copulates with human males.

I am told by an elderly lady that her secrete was unearthed by a young couple who for some odd reason were never affected by field of force that she surrounded herself while it petrified and blinded others. The elders believe it to be a challenge from her father. This couple choused such mundane place for romantic rendezvoused.

They were so immersed in passion and love that jina Nyima was deliriously delighted watching them carry on, kiss, laugh, act frisky, mischievous, and at times crying over each other's shoulders.

The jinni was amorous and affixed by the pantomime that unfolds before her from humanoids in love. In this of panoply of a paradoxical state paralleled to nonexxxxx the jinni queen is entertained. It represented a cavalcade of paroxysms in her life.

In one hand she would instantly turn those who venture to cross the line at the periphery of Bere Kolong into stones for invading her territory. On the other hand this human couple was a source of joy and relief from normal jinni panoplies. It was a parody by which this pariah jinni takeoff her shoulders cumbersome load imposed upon her by jinni Musa. To make certain of this entertainment, which by the way varies daily and always leaves her heart laden with love, envy, and a wish that she too was a human instead of the jinni race she belonged she rendered the couple immune to the spell around her sphere.

Some villagers reported that the Jinni queen and her human lover do at times change into human forms and adorned the most fancy dresses and join the villagers in their festivities, christenings, thanks giving, and even during burial rites.

This jinni was one with human heart encased in a spirit that refuses to be with its kind. At the same time if any human makes the wrong move to wooing her mate she is dealt with immediately. How do the innocent distinguish these icy hands of the stone hedges from real people? It so happens that one look at the couple reveals the tell tales of uniqueness not seen in any in the gathering.

They look perfect in features, youthful despite notable advancing age, they still retain teenage voices and they behave very maturely while saying very little at all. They are normally interested in the elderly and children but maintain short conversations with them. Hence this attribute leaves people suspicious and circumspect at all times when such figurines are in attendants.

Above all, one or two well respected oracle or soothsayers would normally issue warnings to the likely hood that the couple may per chance appear at such gatherings well before the chosen date of the function. However, their presence was never the dooms day or as bleak as the oracles normally predicts.

At the middle or end of each function the jinni couple donates bags upon bags of money and clothing to the organizers and villagers leaving everyone happy and in welcoming spirit. The only missing part of the jigsaw is that there is that neither a village nor known address exists for this philanthropic couple. Amazingly al the villagers notice at the end of visit is sudden appearance of power cyclone marking their disappearance to Batutadou before eventually returning to Bere Kolong. In the end the villagers learnt to live with this phenomenon and those who bore baby boys leave the environment believing that might safe their boy from being kidnapped by the jinni. They run to neighbors and relatives at villages hundreds of miles away until their child matures.I am told that this activity of kidnapping and breeding with ceased males continued for millenniums until one night when a ball of fire was seen to rise to the sky leaving behind it row after row of petrified and chard stones in human form or figurines surrounding Bere Kolong. Some believe it to mark the death of the queen jinni daughter of Jinni Musa.Up to today visitors to Bere Kolong could see stones, in similar fashion to the stone hedges, standing alongside the great Bere Kolong. Some observers reported spotting one or two tears weeping while other figurines drone a smile at beholders. All in all and unto the present time no villager dares draw water from Bere Kolong for fear of angering the mutant jinni she left behind. One good thing about the place is that modern day man had taken advantage and has turned the well into a tourist Mecca generating revenues for the villages and the region. This then was the gift from the most bazaar romantic affair between jinni and man. The saying all is well that ends well hold true for this story the queen jinni love.

Grandma Aminata on Pregnancy

Today the topic at the Bantaba was a muted one as it involved more or less women than men. Unlike grandpa Bajoja, Grandma Aminata Kassa was a shy to almost reclusive sweet person. However, when it comes to the Bantaba forum she lights up brighter than the Northern start in the firmament.

On this day she decided to talk on a very exciting and challenging phase in a woman's life. She went straight for the bull's eyes saying, "Pregnancy is the zenith of love and most rewarding of all romantic and erotic relationships. It is an endowment only the female gender experiences.

We are so lucky that men do not get pregnant." This comment drew in loud laughter and support from young and old ladies who nodded in approval. The men refused to remain silent. One man asked, "Do women get pregnant in absence of men? Are we not the key to pregnancy in women?"

This remark angered some women and a few in the audience with a little knowledge of biology retorted, "Pregnancy in reality connotes the scenario of the egg and the chicken. Which one came first?

The sperm and the ovum are all prerequisite to a woman becoming pregnant. Hence none is more significant than the other". The women in support clapped the loudest. It was at this juncture that the sage lady of the day intervened and said, "Both are indeed significant but more so is it for the female who carries the evolution to full term and parturition of the new entity.

Men cannot claim responsibility for this phase; hence part plaid by women is more significant in procreation as without them there will not be any more new and vibrant forms of human life." This remark generated another sarcastic comment from an 80-year-old male in the audience.

He stated, "We men set you restless and give you the joy of your lives and so you are tailored to nurture children for us." A young lady in the crowd yelled, "Not for you in a million years!" The man looked at her directly, laughed and said, "Child watch your mouth and ask your auntie whom you were trying to embarrass.

It may teach you to think twice before opening up your mouth." The girl apologized and sat quietly for the rest of the debate on pregnancy. Well, well, any time the genders gather there seem to surface the question of who is the dominant one among the two and yet, I dare say we cannot live happily without the other.

Grandma having heard from all sides and having given enough chance for debate between the genders told us, "From the day Eve made Adam to eat the forbidden fruit women embarked on a spiraling challenging path. Pregnancy is not a simple single-phase affair.

It has body and mind as well as hormonal and gustatory changes that pregnancy causes most women to endure. One of the most difficult phases was for few unfortunate ones severe vomiting endlessly up to the 10th week of pregnancy and beyond. This has a devastating effect on both mother and child to be."

She warned that, "Women should plan for the event when young and able and not allow pregnancy to occur when old. Pregnancy requires strength, patience and perseverance to cope with the changing phases of the mother and growing baby.

The nourishment demands of the new baby makes us eat like hungry Elephants and leave us ballooning and with an unbearable craving for more food. The weight gains makes us look like an inflated giant caterpillar tier, the kicking and turning movements of the baby as it position itself can be nerving for first time pregnant women.

None of our preferred dresses fit and our hormonal changes go out of hand to making some pregnant women turn into a temporal wild beast as they become irritable, angry at their male partner for delivering them into such confusion and inability to cope with their usual life style.

The experience could be made worst from complication of drugs or disease and when the mature baby starts descending. A series of short contraction heralding labour commences earlier in the third trimester of the pregnancy.

The most challenging moments of this forty-two weeks or less of ups and down encountered during pregnancy, is the last two hours when painful uterine contractions of increasing strength accompanied by breaking of water commonly known as a show, and dilatation to allow passage of the baby's head in parturition.

This is the most difficult and cause of many would be mothers loss their lives along with their pretty babies." During this explanation the crowd was as silent as midnight in the middle of the Sahara Desert. It scared a few of the young ladies and couples and reminded the menopausal their day and encounter of the first time they went into labour.

Grandma asked, "Why in the dickens do we still repeat this deadly experience over and over without hesitation or fear of what may happen to us?" The only answer she said, "lies wholly and solely on love and love of holding our own unique replica.

It is not about proving our love to our husbands or lovers, for they will chicken out after the first term of pregnancy and will never allow such experience to occur in their life for any price offered.

We repeatedly get pregnant for love and because nature assigned such coveted role only to women of the species. And we do carry it out with gusto and joy of having children in our lives." She ended the debate by advising ladies not to get pregnant when they are sick or old. These make them vulnerable and may risk theirs' and life of their unborn babies in so doing.

Day of the Matchmaker

Matchmakers like people in search of a call are normally caught in a wild fire of passion to help free lonely hearts from the grip of fear and in so doing enables others to enter the magical romantic world. This type of help comes in as a call to matchmakers.

Most matchmakers are in one-way or the other are themselves lonely but rather push others into relationship than daring the social waves of maturity. They are desperately in love but could not make the first move to fulfil their impulses.

Some matchmakers do it for monetary gains. Hence they go head over heels to get others hooked. The matchmaker is extremely gratified when he or she succeeds in bringing love to others. Hence let us observe matchmaker Malang Bulafema and how he brought the coupling of Fafanding Fatajo and Miss Umie Pullo of sare Jarga village, Lower Badibou, the Gambia, West Africa.

Events had it that Malang Bulafema and Fafanding Fatajo met after a day's work in the fields and where on the way home when they accidentally ran across Miss Umie Pullo. Umie is a beautiful twenty-three year old longhaired Fulani girl.

Malang instantly noted Fafangding's conversation stuttering and his gazed fixated on the girl. Sensing something very deep about the look Malang tested the waters by asking Fafanding if she was gorgeous and how he felt about her. He pushed his luck by asking if Fafanding would like her to be his wife.

Both questions took Fafanding by surprise knowing that Malang Bulafema was known in the village as master news monger and who most keep their secretes away from him to avoid being the talk of the day at the village Bantaba.

Because of this laxity in Malang he was able to gain access into private yearnings of many villagers especially young women whose confidence he had more than most in the region. Elders fear him with their daughters, as he was perceived as the right hand of modern day Satan.

Matchmakers were in those days perceived as people working for none other than the Devil and Satan. Malang was instantly challenged by Fafanding's refusal to answer any of the above-posed questions to him. He knew that Fafanding's fancy has been tickled and he must continue searching for the threshold of Fafanding's pulses and his feelings about Umie Pullo.

Umie Pullo is one of the darlings of Sare Jarga village. She is courteous, very self-respecting, hardworking, and gorgeous young lady that any normal male would like her as a wife. No wonder her parents and elders of the village were mighty proud of her and the way she carried herself.

Neither Fafading nor Umie ever had lovers but had many peer friends full of admiration for them. So would bringing this two untouched be a challenge or not? Malang had his foolproof plans on how to do exactly that. Having had his inclination as to how Fafanding felt by his refusal to answer question about Umie he turned on to finding Umie's views on men and who would be suitable for her as an ideal life partner.

First he surreptitiously interviewed several known friends of Umie and learnt that beside respect for men Umie hardly had expressed anything of concrete desire about being enamoured or even having a secrete lover at heart. She was according to her friends an angel in human flesh which opinion made lots of her peers sort advice from her and respected her views.

She was through and through an honest young lady who hated lairs and loved her community. Malang had his work cut out for him for these two were the most challenging for him to turn into lovebirds. One thing he was certain was that it would be easier to penetrate Fafanding than Umie's heart.

He next befriended Umie's elder sister to gain more insight into the family and parental control if there was any behind Umie's strict no nonsense life style. The family welcomed him guardedly amongst them but kept their lips tight to avoid being quoted at the Bantaba the next day, week or months later for Malang Bulafema had a knack of getting information he wanted while his victims are unaware of being too gregarious.

Alas! Malang had now collected all the data he wished at his fingertips and went to work for his goal. At first most thought that Umie might have fallen for Malang Bulafema to allow or explain the open-door policy the family recently accorded him.

Only he knew that not to be the case while he continued to lead all astray or on wild goose chases. This suspicious closeness to Umie made one of her Uncles to interrogate Malang Bulafema about his recent closeness to the Pullo family and what were his objectives.

Being under the spotlight he confesses to having no desire or stake on Umie or any of the Pullo female members of the family but had some great news they and him would smile for at the end of the day. Malang Bulafema told his interrogator that it was too soon to spill the beans out but needed a few more moves before he could open up the Pandora's Box.

Her uncle welcomed the findings and was, like the rest, more delighted and curious about what good news this undeclared broadcaster had on their beautiful girl.
Umie was called to a family secret meeting to let the cat out of the bag.

Umie assured them that she had no hidden secrete and was not keeping any from them nor does she know what Malang Bulafema had in mind. Her innocent candor made them even wonder more as to what good news Malang implied when he met with Umie's uncle.

Malang of all people now knows he has to tread his path gingerly in bringing the good news he promised about Umie. Hence he went to work on Fafanding to enable him peak up courage and tell how he felt about Umie.

Lo and behold Fafanding Fatajo had no one in mind other than this lovely Fulani girl Umie. It took Malang quite a juggling act to get Fafanding confess his inner yearning for any girl more so to admit love for this self carrying lady of Sare Jarga.

It came to light that the inclination started as far back as when Umie and Fatajo were tending sheep in the grassland at which time they actually sized each other but never came to giving in for pride and fear of defiling the names of their respective families.

Umie had once made some sort of move in teasing him any time they chance to meet but it never went beyond that village style of romance. They never held hand, kissed or were ever alone together as such proximity at their age was taboo.

Fafanding had opened up to a distant uncle who died before fulfilling his promise of having a family meeting about his yearnings. Hence Fafanding kept his feelings to himself until the day he was walking from the fields accompanied by Malang Bulafema.

He was going to spill the beans out but on realizing Malangs' reputation he backed off to safe guard Umie's feeling for not being told but to hear about her unfounded engagement from nowhere other than the Banataba mouth to mouth broadcasting system.

Malang Bulafema armed with this fantastic success now encircled Umie. One day after the weekly meeting at the Bantaba he cornered Umie and told her of his findings and that Fafanding Fatajo had vowed to marry none other than her. She at first pushed it all aside for fear that Malang was on his rumor gathering tactics.

Three days later she asked one of her friends, Sara Bah, if she heard anything about Fafanding Fatajo and some girl being rumoured in the village. The friend replied in the negative and chuckled at the question with peering eyes at Umie. Both girls laughed and went their ways but her friend became suspicious that Umie herself might be girl she was implying.

The plot thickens as Sara Bah also had an eye on Fafanding Fatajo but his refusal to reciprocate
to her flirting convinced her that Fafanding might be impotent to cause him run away from girls any time he was approached.

Umie asking her about Fafanding made Sara Bah double her attempts to draw Fafanding Fatajos' attention to her before she loses him to other girls in the village specifically Umie.Malang on knowing this brewing battle of the brood decided to bring to Umie's attention the likelihood that her very best and trusted friend Sara Bah was about to steal the jewel of her heart right in front of her very eyes in bright day break.

This infuriated Umie, as love being blind and jealousy it mortal foe. The two girls had an honest confrontation about poor Fafanding Fatajo who remained unaware of battle being waged in his name.This was the key moment Malang Bulafema prayed for as it added his leverage over both Umie Pullo and Fafanding Fatajo.

Now that he knew Umie's willingness to not to give Fafanding away Malang arrange a secret meeting without letting Umie or Fafanding knowing that the two will now be face to face now be offered a face to face chance of speaking out their mind about the other or loosed forever from forest pray lurking in the woods.

Malang made sure he and Fafanding were at the meeting venue earlier than time he gave to Umie Pullo. She arrived with her head covered for fear of being seen with Malang in the bush. She was surprised at seeing Fafanding and almost dashed away out of shyness.

It was Fafanding who politely begged her to stay for them to hear what Maland had to say and why he brought them together in this unusual manner. She agreed after gathering her nerves and said, "Go on tell us why this meeting and of all places it could take place".

She loved Fafanding and was not about to miss the chance to talk things with him in this and time. She is acutely aware of competition brewing up between her and Sara

Bah, which she was determined to stamp out and cut it at the bud before an irreversible mistake occours. Malang asked Fafanding to open up and be a man by repeating what he told him about this Umie girl before the two of them and God.

Fafanding Fatajo with eyes on the ground, barely able to look into Umie's faces directly, at first stuttered and then said, "Yes, Umie it's true I love you with all my heart and would feel blessed if you acquiesces to that wish of you becoming my wife following traditional norms".

Umie was filled with joy and tears of delight ran down her cheeks. She ran to hug him and said, "I too feel blessed having you my husband and future father of our children". It is said that a way to man's heart is through his stomach but a bouquet of red roses with a diamond engagement ring inserted in it is sure way to catch a girl.

Well, Malang Bulafema has capped one more romantic success in his commitment of bringing love to seesawing hearts. The meeting resulted for the first time the pair walked holding hands until at the fringes of the village before Fafanding Fatajo told her that his Uncle Sheriff Balajo and friends would soon start the ball rolling for their final union as man and wife.

On reaching home umie could hardly wait to tell her mother Hulay Ndong but begged her to keep it as strict secrete until the arrival and meeting of the Pullo family by Sherif Balajo and company. Umie and her mother were delighted in silence knowing what was about to unfold for Umie and the Pullo family.

A week went by before the expected delegates showed up at the door of the Pullo family. Samba Pullo, Umie's father, welcomed the guest and after normal formalities and lots of enquiries about each other's family's' health,

Bachi Pullo, umies' uncle asked the guest what was their mission to cause them call upon the family on that glorious day of the year of love. Sheriff Balajo wasted no time in letting the Pullo family know that they have been asked by their son and nephew Fafanding Fatajo to come and asked for privilege of having the hand of their daughter Umie Pullo in marriage to Fafanding Fatajo. They were given listening ears indicating that Umie had not been a bad girl.

In response Bachi Pullo said, "Let us first take a glass of palm wine as it makes men eloquent and give love to tame women". All laughed after the libation. Bachi Pullo told the delegate that the Pullo family would discuss the good news and wish of their nephew Fafanding Fatajo after consulting Umie Pullo about it.

A reply will be sent through the family scribe in two days. They again greeted, shook hands and Fafanding's envoy departed hopeful and happy they engaged or chosen to marry a family friend.At dinner, Bachi Pullo convened meeting of the elders of the family with Umie, her mother Hulay Ndong, aunts along with elderly ladies who had historical ties with life of the Pullo fraternity.

They were all extremely delighted and honoured hearing the request from Fafanding Fatajo but all agreed that only Umie could, and rightly so, could give the response everyone assembled awaits.

Aunty Awa Pulbe got up, spat the tobacco she filled her mouth up and said "It was her aunty duties to ask the young lady before them if she loves the fellow requesting her hand in marriage knowing that he was no Fulani but a good mandinka." Inter tribal marriages are rare especially between Fulas and the Mandinka.

Hence she must here and now tell them how she feels about this and if need be request time to think but they must know before two days as promised to Sheriff Balajo. Umie Pullo got up and bravely addressed her father, mum, aunts and elderly friend of the clan.

She told them, "I was more delighted than any of you for this was light at the end of tunnel and have been praying for God to grant the wish that she would meet a man she loves and loves her in return. Fafanding Fatajo's heart and hers' were intertwined into one soul.

She loves him dearly would marry him right away if the family bless her wish and request". She requested their indulgence and sat down and waited for formal approval from her family.

The clan was happy to hear her wish and have blessed it unreservedly because Fafanding Fatajo was well liked in the village and his family not only being historical friends of the Pullos but had always come to their aid if needed and attend and participated in any event involving the Pullo family.

Hence, without any objection is raised by all present, Bachi Pullo told her "We conquer with you and pray that this union of hearts and friendship yield even more fruitful rearwards for the two families. Samba Gaulo, the Pullo family scribe, was then asked to report the outcome to Sheriff Balajo and the Fatajo family so that discussions could start on the dowry and setting of the wedding date.

 Early in the morning of the next day Samba Gaulo and an assistant priest went to tell Sheriff Balajo of the good news that the Pullo family gladly acquiescent to his nephew Fafanding Fatajo marrying Umie Pullo and that his side should now arrange for time of discussions pertaining to the dowry and setting of the wedding date. Sheriff told Samba Gaulo, "Kindly convey our joy in hearing their response to our hearts' desire and to tell the Pullo family that the Fatajos were more than delighted for this continuing gesture of friendship and trust and that discussions would start sooner than expected after he conveys this fantastic news to all concerned.

Africa being steep in tradition allows cordial ironing out of important matters in the family, among friends and even with adversaries. The family met and agreed on a set dowry to discuss knowing the Pullo family like cattle more than diamonds. Friday a week after consultations the two families met at the home of a respected village elder to debate, iron out differences and arrive at mutually acceptable dowry to enable marriage of Umie Pullo and Fafanding Fatajo. It

was at the end agreed that the Fatajo family pay a dowry of twenty cattle, twenty bushels of maze, ten goats, and loads of dresses and presents Umie would demand. This was considered reasonable knowing the attachment of Fulani's to animals.

The more cattle they boast about the more social standing they become. In short is power and this was the best time to get as much of it as can be before the nut is tied between Umie and Fafanding.The Western minded would cry out foul in believing that the whole fiasco was a deal selling Umie and never catered her interest.

In Africa parents love their children and do break their backs for them during their growing days. In addition marrying away does not end the relationship or the family's contribution to the welfare of the kids as happens in foreign cultures.

Hence the stronger their stand at old age the better they can continue to be of help. Dowries are considered as the child's part contribution to what the Western people recognizes or call pensions reward for the family. The cattle and goats can always be sold at hard times.

Certain numbers of the animals are normally earmarked for the bride in the event she may need help due to poor yield or for treatment of some sort. Barring the surfacing of any objection or any reasonable alibis for annulment and dowry being paid the date for the wedding is set.

The village scribe, town crier according to Western cultures, is asked to announce the good news to all in the village, hamlets and others far and wide as possible to draw maximum participation in the ceremony.

A Friday is selected and the elders, priest along with the two families, friends and celebrants all join in to anoint the marriage between Fafanding Fatajo and Umie Pullo before the eye of God and her parents. Now both peers of the couple pitch in to help the preparation for the forthcoming wedding ceremony.

The fellow's family, brothers, sisters, aunts and companions all pitch in to make it a memorable wedding festivities and night to remember. Upon the completion of the mosque activities the bride and groom are allowed visitation and his friends usually accompany the groom.

On the day of the real marriage ceremony the whole village and nearly all the neighbouring villages gather to participate in the event. Umie in her tribe's bridal dress and costume becomes envy of her lady peers. There is drumming and dancing all day until late in the evening before the bride enters the grooms house accompanied by elderly village women.

The husband or his friends help her cross the so-called threshold. The friends leave them alone for the night. The ecstasy this night of the honeymoon and day could never be matched by any other occasion other than the birth of a child. The couple can now stay permanently together, for better or worse as husband and wife.

The ceremony usually continues up to dawn before the younger celebrants retire. The bride keeps on her bridal attire for at least two weeks before shedding them for good. Most women store these special dresses for life, giving them only to their daughters if they cannot get their own.

The saying that, my wife is mine and I do with her what I want does not exist in a village setting. Here, family and community are the basic fibre of life. Hence, there are a host of irreconcilable differences between traditional Mandinka cultures and their western counterparts.

Malang Bulafema let a shy of relief having bagged this union of hearts in his archives and was triumphant in telling Bachi Pullo that what he just witnesses about Umie was due to his relentless effort and believes that these two lovebirds were tailor made for each other.

He wished them a happy marriage life and the best of health in days, weeks and years to come. Pullo stood in amazement abound with the highest regards for persistence and sense of worthy purpose as exhibited by Malang Bulafema in the above saga.

It made him now disagree with all the rumours about this matchmaker and let the scene happy that it all end well for both sides and people were dead wrong about Malang the matchmaker of the day at Sare Jarga.

Bushland Love

Sare Toro Tayem is located in the woody area near the fringiest of the Dobo Forest some twenty miles from Manding Medical Center. At Njawara two doctors, Massembe Bah and Yoro Jalo shared a surgery for many years and had become the icon of private practice in the region.

Nurse Adama Jange and Dr. Massembe were total strangers who now have to work at the Medical center at Njawara. Adam, a fully-qualified Staff Nurse, had leaved in Banjul, Gambia's capital, all her life and had never ventured or been to bush country nor did she ever come across Hyenas, Leopards, or seen life Antelopes roaming freely in mother nature's garden in the Savanna.

Being city born she was frightened to death by crawling insects, snakes and lizards which undoubtedly will soon become among her regular guests' asides humans. None the less Nurse Adam Jange opted to follow her instinct and applied to work at the Manding Medical Centre three hundred miles in the hinter land.

It was away from trappings of city life, neon lights, noisy motor cars and trucks plying to and fro to undefined destinations of commerce, restaurants and endless social amenities that she knew all her life but have to leave behind.Dr. Massembe had decided to give her ride on his way back to the hospital at Manding Medical Centre in Njawara.

In a jovial manner he asked her, "You do understand the danger in your decision?" Nurse Jange frowned at him making him feel embarrassed and thoughtless for trying to frighten the dickens out of a young lady determined to provide invaluable service to communities no other contemporary of her would want to go. In her mind she has her own questions about the air of

mystry and charm that lurked in the man seating besides her asking silly boyish question and attempting to frighten her in other to have a conversation with her. She told him, "Do not worry for one of her uncle's traded in Njawara for thirty years and spoke well of the people and the beauty of the Savannah."
She told him lot of things had changed since his death. She broke off as a sob rose in her throat. After three years the memory of her adored uncle who had died suddenly and tragically in a road traffic accident in that same remote bush country, still brought painful tears to her eyes.

Dr. Massebe let her know they will leave the next day. Her eyes shone with determination. She told him, "I want to go as soon as possible now that the Royal Victoria Hospital has released me there was no reason for any delay when there was so much to do in Njawara".
She added that she even have her personal luggage down to a toothbrush and a change of shirts and underwear ready.
The next day at the arranged time Dr. Massembe arrived dressed as if heading to a VIP party. As he stepped out the van Nurse Jange looked round curious to see the stranger with whom she would soon be working so closely at the Manding Medical Centre in bush country. He looked thirty some odd years she guessed.
He was tall and fair, as most Fulanies, and his body was lean and muscular. His eyes weighed her up again but this time much more than the last time and his thin Fulani lips

in a solemn face relaxed into a faint smile in his attempt to maintain the doctor nurse protocol. Nurse Adam Jange entered and sat at the passenger side while Dr. Massembe took to his driver's seat with Adam throwing or stealing a glance or two at his clean-
shaven profile adorned with aroma of the best perfume there was at the time. He was certainly her ideal man and was very good looking she thought in silence. Dr. Massembe broke the silence by telling Nurse Jange, "The Manding Medical Centre considers itself lucky to have her among its cadre of nurses.
Your uncle worked so hard helping the villagers. We are delighted for your joining the team and they shook hands. He reminded her of being told about the hardships that lie ahead at the Medical center."
He told her the farmers and especially the children were suffering terribly from famine and disease and the countryside and the recent creeping of the Sahara desert in the Sahel region has devastated farms. From the sound of what he just said,
Adam thought him to be a warm and compassionate man and she felt she would enjoy working with him. She now kept wondering if this man was married. She chuckled at the thought that she was wondering about the private life of a stranger she just met for the first time.
In flashed memory of the last paragraph in letter her uncle sent her before the accident came to her mind. "Dear Adam Jange, I have been busy lately as I had to send a convoy of food that was desperately needed by the villagers.
The harvest had been poor this season. Sometimes we must do our best for these unfortunate farmers. They do appreciate our effort in their behalf.

If only there was more food, more medicines and supplies, and more medical personnel to help cope with the demand. Perhaps young boys and girls will join the medical profession and head to serve such places, as I am currently located."

It was that paragraph in the letter that helped her make up her mind about joining the medical center at Njawara. She had been thinking for some time of going out to her uncle and help in his work. Her father and mother died long ago when she was barely twelve years old, but throughout her childhood her uncle had been there for her.

He even paid all her education and nursing training school fees and uniforms along buffered it with a fat monthly allowance. The trip to Njawara would take almost three days drive over dusty bumpy roads but she was ready for the experience and would savour it to the fullest.

"So sorry about your uncle Dr. Massebe said even though I never intended to revive emotions from you but just to strike a conversation over the long and tedious journey to Njawara". He now understood why she wanted to serv at the medical centre at Njawara in bush land.

After four and half hours of dusty roads the vehicle stopped and Dr. Massembe escorted her to one of best of the best local Pasuar/ restaurant for a rest and delicious benechin commonly known as Jolof rice. It was only at this restaurant that the magic spells of woodland romance reared its head in their hearts.

A beautiful sunset greeted them and smiling face of the staff added a décor to it all. The place was clean and staff/girls not only appear immaculate but also were beautiful. Their smiles and winks made Adam Jange's heart percolate with jealousy for fear that the lovelies would steer her man away even though they were yet to be exposed. Clumsily she filled herself and had cocoa drink and pulls a purse in attempt to pay for her share of the meal. At which time Dr. Massembe genteelly held hand and stopped her giving money to the waitress.

He said, "Today is my turn for I know how you women libbers perceive men nowadays." This infuriated her but at the same time made her happy that he was not about to yield his machismo to a female with little money at hand. They took off and drove to Mansa konko where they each took different rooms at headquarters of the divisional commissioner for the night.

Commissioner Tubab Davis treated them generously. The next day an early breakfast was prepared for them before they set off for next leg of the journey to Njawara. This time the two spoke freely and frequently while checking the social profiles of the other.

Hence Nurse Adam Jange found that Dr. Massembe being a book worm never had chance to marry and had since returning from his medical training in the Uk settled at Njawara more concerned about plight of the villager little he could get out of social shoulder rubbing.

He does not hate women nor does he shun them but he just never made up his mind to be involved with any yet. He leaves alone in bungalow at the medical centre. As for Nurse Adam Jange, she was born and breathes as city girl. She had all her schooling in Banjul.

She did had the normal high school romances here and there but nothing serious nor was she ever involved with men since she took up nursing. She now heads to fulfil a long standing dream of hers, which is to carry the torch her uncle lit for the down trodden villagers.

Every hour they spent seem to draw them closer as the veil of uncertain was gradually removed. Their next stop was at Janjanbure, a former home have returned slaves from America, now headquarters of Central Division.

Again the commissioner matched the previous one at Mansa Konko in displaying hospitality to them. Again, they took different room but ate together seated side by side unlike at the restaurant.

Lot of stories were heard from the commissioner about the area and of wild animals creeping into his bed room if the servants got careless to forget to luck the backs doors before darkness. By midnight the two visitors bide each other a good night full of sweet dreams and went straight for their designated rooms.

This time sleep did not come easy to both of them as they started ruminating about the other and where does it all head to. Would relationship materialized or was it a spur of the moment thing? Dr. Massembe was uncertain as to the fact that Nurse Adam Jange might just see another she falls for.

He was going to take his time for as long as it need to be certain of her feeling for him with making any move or signalling his heart's yarning for her. Adam too was concern about his aloofness but happy that it kept him away from other ladies but that would not deter her archiving wining him over in due course.

She did not feel like sleeping but afraid to walk out she stretched her feet at the corridor in the humidity of the night with bright skies and adorned by stars. There was constant humming of birds with strange creatures passing afar but she could not identify them.

Looking further down the corridor she saw what looked like Dr. Massebe with some papers over deem light. At first she wanted to walk straight to him but that would make her look cheap and give him the upper edge of affairs.

She held against her emotions and held her pride but did what most women do in trying to attention of a mate. She deliberately dropped the teacup she decided to pick up from her room to the corridor.

Soon the watchman, the commissioner and of course the great doctor Masambe were at her side enquiring as to what went wrong and why was she not in bed that late of the night. She turned away meaning to go back to her room but love overcame her and she plopped into the strong hands of the doctor.

Both he and the commissioner took her to her bed and comforted her. She thank the men assured them se was ok but would like the doctor stay a while to keep an eye over her. She was not certain why she felt.

Dr. Masembe got very worried and concern that she might be an epileptic or had some voodoo cast upon her by jealous competitor females. Whatever the case he was determined to get to the bottom of it before it become too late for both of them. The others left after ten minutes leaving only Nurse Adam and DR. Massembe together in the room.

She sprung to her feet as soon as she was certain that the others were sound asleep in their rooms and told Dr. Massembe that there was nothing wrong with her and that the whole affair was an act she did to call his attention but the noise from the teacup got out of proportion to draw the attention of the others for which she was sorry.

He understood and asked her not to apologies for he too could not sleep for the thought of her and their future. At that statement tears of joy dripped down the cheeks of Nurse Adam causing Dr. Massembe to uncontrollably lick them up clean from her face.

They embraced for the first time solemnly promising to keep each other forever and ever. "My love is yours forever", Dr. Massembe told the nurse clutched in his arms with him feeling her heart beat second by second. He set her to bed and left for his own room.

Very soon the telephone rang and the two picked up where they left in conversation, which went through the wee hours of the night. The commissioner was the first to visit sleepy Adam to find out how things went and whether she would need transport to take her back to the Royal Victoria hospital for further check up and examination.

She assured him of no need for that and they would proceed to their destination, Manding Medical Centre. The host left a bit worried but relived knowing she was a nurse with a doctor in suitor. Soon doctor and nurse were at breakfast throwing more romantic glances interwoven with smiles that petrify the beholder.

They were both at cloud nine in their hearts as they have found each other and would try to keep it for life barring premature death. They took off and held hands throughout the rest of the journey with other warning of fears of losing their grip.

After three days and almost twenty hours of dusty bumpy roads the van came to creaking stop at the bungalow of none other than Dr. Massembe. Children and caretakers of the place dashed to welcome him back.

The kids told him how pleased they were for he had finally brought his wife with him. The girl said, "Welcome home mum and would you like coffee or tea and bread with it?" Adam Jange was not sure what to say but went along and said, "Yes if doctor will join me to a late mornings' cup of tea."

Dr. Massembe had his luggage unloaded from the van and he drove two streets away to Flat number 245 the new home of Nurse Adam Jange. Alas! She made it to Njawara. More than anything is she looked forward to meeting the hospital administrators and getting acquainted with the wards, patients, staff and not the least residents of Njawara.

She spruced up and looked at her pretty face while accidentally speaking to the mirror for a while. She finally threw herself to the bed for a few minutes relaxation after such long and tiring journey to Njawara. She tried to close her eyes but the images of Massembe would not leave her free.

She went to the already supplied kitchen and poured herself some milk in warm chocolate and drank it slowly. She turned the FM Radio and had familiar voices of the Banjul Theatre. Right then she felt home sick and asked if her resignation from the Royal Victoria Hospital was not premature and spur of the moment decision.

She finally concluded that it was too late to change her mind and besides she wanted to do work like this for the down trodden and no place deserve her service. Also a bonus in the form of Dr. Messembe was now certain for her. Only a fool would turn her back from such opportunity to serve and be loved inclusively.

It was not until after six pm did Dr. Massembe called to check on her and told her that he decided to give her few moments for rest and reflection. She was happy to hear him and the conversation went on for hours as if they were teenagers not known when to hang up the phone.

He cautioned her that they must move slowly to avoid rumourmongers etc. She retorted and asked if he was hiding from a girl friend in the region. Dr. Massembe emphasized that the tradition of the region is different from big city Banjul and that he wants people to respect her and not see her as a swinger.

She understood about concerns he expressed and promised not to go off guard. They then had a long goodbye kiss and retired for the night. The first thing Nurse Adam noticed was the braying of the donkeys intermingled with sporadic howls of hyenas.

This scared the dickens out of her and made her first night away from big city Banjul traumatic. She hardly slept for fear that these animals will jump through her window and have her as a rare snack. It was almost dawn orchestrated by the sounds of cocks all over the village.

She could not wait for day brake to tell Dr. Massembe of her first night at Njawara. She had her breakfast and headed for the admin building to meet Matron Ramatulie Jarala Ceesay. Ram as the staff knew her, was a cheerful cheery individual who welcomed Nurse Adam.

After a brief chat they headed to the wards for Adam to meet the staff and see things in reality at Manding Medical Centre. Sister Jainaba, the in-charge of Female Surgical was the first they met. There was a warm handshake and welcome to Female surgical.

They walked through and as they pass patients Adam thought, without saying it loud, that there was so much to do for the patients manned by so skeletal a staff number. Some of the younger male patients watched with interest as she went from bed to bed.

These sceneries were repeated throughout the hospital complex and ancillary units. She was overwhelmed by the cheerfulness and hard working staff she met. Things were not like that at her ward at the Royal Victoria Hospital in Banjul where she worked since becoming a nurse.

She loved the atmosphere and team spirit of her new place. Manding Medical Centre was good choice and place to work indeed. On returning to Matron's office she was given the regular uniform of the hospital and asked to take the rest of the weekend off to familiarize herself with Njawara and the shops.

She starts duty at the Paediatrics' ward on Monday. She was delighted for her love of children made her specialized in paediatric nursing. No sooner than reaching her flat did she call Dr. Massembe, enquired about his day, asked if he missed her and spilled the beans of being very happy that she came and that she was much impressed by the staff and cleanliness of the hospital in general.

She was looking forward to start at the Paediatric ward on Monday. Doctor Massembe summarized his day as being very hectic with lot of surgical cases and that the male surgical ran out of beds. Unlike Banjul, which has mixed wards, Manding Medical Centre prides itself in keeping the genders apart for respectability and comfort of the patient.

This was another aspect that Adam noticed and liked about her new hospital. Despite the rush of things he did miss being by her side etc. He invited her to dine with him at his Bungalow after 7:00 pm, which she accepted unhesitatingly for she was itching to be kissed by his sweet lips once more. The table was set for two by the time she arrived.

A bouquet of bougainvilleas flowers welcomed her at the door and after jointly listening and watching the evening news the couple migrated to the dining table to fill themselves with delicious Domoda and Njar Meu drinks. Neither of them partake alcohol or spirits but coca cola and Fantail took waves.

Having filled their Tummies they moved to the couch and watched video drama plays, in each other's arms, by Senegalese, Gambian and Nigerian artists until well after midnight before she retired to her flat very happy indeed. She revels in these dramas on local daily chitchats and romantic stories.

The visit ended at midnight for Doctor. Massembe has a full schedule of operations, which start 7:00 Am prompt. They said goodbye and she went home very elated. For some reason the sounds of the night never border her as it did in her first night.

Hence, she slept soundly like a log until 9:00 am when the maid showed up to clean the flat. The next day being Saturday; she got up late and had a quick bath and breakfast to allow the young lady do her daily chores. She then took a walk to main town Njawara's shopping centre. You guessed it. She stole the show for being the new tantalizing girl in the block.

She had so much attention she never bargained for. Men and elderly women praised her for coming to help and even expressed admiration of her petrifying beauty.Their presence sent jitters into hearts of young ladies who feared losing their men to her for she was a magnet to men. Having seen most of the shopping malls and done her own bit of shopping, she walked away from the metropolitan sector of Njawara.

Soon she reached collections of mud huts built about in open space with no fencing around them. Smoke bellowing from half a dozen huts rose lazily into the still hot air. A dozen or so of women and children eyed her as she finds her way around the huts.

Nurse Jange saw an innocent looking four year old boy who was sucking his thumb walked towards her. He smiled and held her hand and said, "Welcome to our village miss". He had huge red eyes in a sunken face with pathetically thin arms staring at her.

Nurse Adam Jange asked if they were all this malnourished. The boy's legs seem hardly able to support his swollen potbelly. At the end tears sprang to nurse's eyes. She had heard of stories of hunger in the region but never dreamt it to be this devastating.

The sight of the little boy gave her more resolve strength to work at the paediatric ward for the rest of her life or stay at Mamding Medical Centre. She would contact international agents such as UNESCO for relief in their behalf and she vowed to work to help these beleaguered children.

Dr. Massembe was more than delighted to hear her reaction to the plight and need for help in the region and promised to do all he could to let the chief executive bless her projects for the region's children.

Both Doctor and nurse spent most of the day indoor at their residents. Doctor was finalizing lecture he was to deliver to the medical students doing their electives at Manding Medical Centre and nurse had decided to take it easy and take in the change that met her since leaving big city Banjul.

They spoke briefly over the phone and then let the rest of the day find its path. Monday marked the first day of duty at the paediatric ward for Nurse Jange. She arrived twenty minutes early and made good impressions on the sister on duty who was happy about her. She greeted everyone and along with the rest of the staff took over the ward from the night team.

It all went smoothly for its repetition of her daily life at the Royal Victoria Hospital in Banjul. The junior staff and auxiliaries loved her simplicity and ability to lead without being implosive. The young doctors started showing interest, just as Dr. Massembe feared and had cautioned her on their way to Njawara.

Nonetheless she stuck to her guns and had the young bulls follow hospital protocol and not think they can muscle their way to her heart. She has her eyes and heart already set on Dr. Massembe and would not exchange him for any infatuated male doctor period.

No wonder then the first question coming from Dr. Massembe asked about the young doctors' behaviour toward her. She assured him of having put them in their rightful places and that he; Dr. Massembe was her idol and love. That will not change for any reason other death separating them.

Hearing this much commitment from her pleased doctor Massembe and it boosted his confidence to match forward with head held high. He too reaffirms his undying love for her and promised to marry her as soon as she gets her feet on the ground at Manding Medical Centre. Nurse Adam did exactly what she resolved. Much aid came to the village from various churches and UN organization since the first encounter with potbelly boy at the outskirts of Njawara.

In the wards her work had been superb and lots of good confidential reports and recommendation both from parent of children, nurses and doctors who worked with her, were sent to her file at the Matron's office. It was to no one's surprise of her being automatically nominated to take over the paediatric ward when the current in-charged retire on health grounds.

She became head nurse at the Manding Medical centre's paediatric unit two years after joining the hospital staff. This was rapid promotion indeed and she and Dr. Massembe savoured it very well.

She found Dr. Massembe very helpful indeed but wished her uncle were alive to witness her contributions. In silence, at her flat, she raised a glass full of milk and said, "Uncle this one is for you. Rest happily and know that your torch shall continue to light the path of these people who are touched by its generousness. Cheers!"

Both the district authority and Governor of the region gave awards for job well done and encouraged her to teach other ladies in the Nursing field. Dr. Massembe's parents hail from Kerr Ado a stone throw from Njawara. His father migrated to Banjul in search of greener pastures.

He eventually met and instantly fell in love with Kumba Mokalpoch of Kerr Willan in Dingare ward, Banjul and married her. They had Massembe and two other girls. Now Dr. Massembe had return to his father's native land to provide a much needed medical service to the region. Today he is going to fulfil his father's wish that is to marry and present him a grandchild before he joins God and their ancestors in heaven.

He invited Nurse Adam to his Bungalow and to her greatest surprise, even though she knew he would propose but this day took her by surprised. Hence, after their normal formalities, Dr. Massembe took out a small box and another full of beautiful dresses specially made for Adam and said, "This is for you.

I love you and want you be my wife for life". Adam quickly opened the first small box wrapped with colours of the Gambia and found a pure gold ring in it. Overwhelmed she said, "Yes, I love you and would be the happiest girl in the block being your wife and mother of your children.

May God anion our wish for happiness, health and prosperity together". They kissed again and again as if that was their first in life. He followed tradition by sending his uncles and close friend to approach parents of Adam Jange for her hand in marriage.

The delegation came back with the proposal being accepted and that the Imam, their parents and elders of Banjul will be offering prayers to officially sanction the marriage between them at the Grand Banjul Mosque the following week.

Dr. Massembe drove to Banjul to attend the occasion. Mean while both staff of the Manding medical centre, Njawara and all nearby district went into a massive preparation for the wedding ceremony of the cherished nurse and doctor they ever had. All sorts of presents of ladies embroidery some set aside animals they would donate for slaughter for food during the ceremony.

The semi wealthy bought diamond studded necklaces, gold bangles with matching earrings. The cobblers made special ancient but well decorated pairs of shoes for the bride. The grand day came a month after Dr. Massembe announced that their intending to marriage.

Tribes from the region and afar poured in not only to participate but also to show their gratitude to the couple and also witness another unique occasion for the region. It was rare thing for Banjul born to shorn the glitter of Banjul and have their historic moment celebrated in bush country,

So everyone was elated and danced to their heart's content in marking the true meaning of the day for the couple and celebrants. It was a cheerful and memorable day that none of them would ever forget. The drums, dancing, chanting of scribes was spectacular.

The bride and bridegroom were overwhelmed with bundles upon bundles of presents and animals lined up for slaughter in their behalf. The hospital staff did not lag behind in showing appreciation and generosity to the colleagues in wedding.

None other than the chief executive, matron and the governor of entire region, presented special gifts from the hospital. This then was community in action and display of gratitude and ineptness for kindness shown to the by the couple.

The Governor of the region gave long speeches as what an exemplary thing these couple had been to them all. He praised them over and over and wished them happiness in their lives together. It was a joyous occasion for all he concluded. The region's representative follows with similar line of comments and again paid for the pair's happiness.

The mayor of Njawara spoke in behalf of the villagers and pointed out the impact Nurse Adam Jange and Dr. Massembe had on the life of the villagers especially the children who she worked so hard to have international and UN agents come to their aid.

He was personally indebted to them eternally and would name his next child after Adam if a girl or Dr. Massembe if it turn out to be a male. Everyone laughed but understood the significant of it. It was an honour bestrode to few for such a remarkable Mayor to name one of his after an individual. In addition to the verbal commendations Nurse Adam Jange was handed a citation of appreciations for her service to the region. It read: "In recognition of your outstanding dedication in improving nursing and healthcare delivery.

The City of Njawara proudly bestowed upon its daughter this citation of highest achievement in the field of nursing and service to the region. Nurse Adam Jange has in many times put everything second including her family. She works hard for delivery of medicine to villagers especially children."

The ceremony went on until late at night before the celebrants retired to bed. The next day the couple flew to America for a two months holiday. They returned to their jobs two months late but with Adam carrying triplets for Dr. Massemble. She refused maternity leave until two weeks to her due day before taking rest to prepare for the arrival of the babies. Her instinct for call of nursing dwarfs that of most people.

An Ode to Love

Love, an instinct of adoration innate to man, is a unique phenomenon that almost sacrifices one heart to another. It is an adoration that touches the heart beyond any yearning. Love is the force that melts hearts into one and yet leaves the individuals intact.

Love causes a mother who cannot swim to plunge head long into a raging river to safe her drowning child knowing she could drown with him. The embers of love keep us fired and restless about another. Love remains the most mystical relationship that can develop between two strangers.

For the love of you I would give my heart as token of friendship one suitor told his future bride. Love is blind but the lover can never lose sight of the one that caught his or her fancy. Love and instinct is what causes ladies to go through pregnancy and risk of labour over and over till menopause.

Love makes us affectionate, attractive and beautiful at heart. It is the most pleasant and devotional feeling one can have for another human being. It is a chemistry of the heart and mystery, which alchemists could not explain. Love is what makes the voice of one's lover sound like melodious music that none utters other than our lovers. Love has fuelled our partnerships since recorded times. Love is our passions' slave.

In biblical resonance Corinthian chapter 13, verses 4 – 8 it speaks of love thus: Love is patients. Love is kind. It does not envy, it does not boast, it is not proud, it is not rude and it is not self-seeking. Love is not easily angered and it keeps no record of wrongs. Love dose not delight in evil but rejoices with truth.

It always protects, always trusts, always hopes and always preserves. Love never fails. William Shakespeare in Romeo and Juliet said of love as my bounty is as boundless as the sea. My love as deep, the more I give to thee the more I have, for both are infinite.

Love is indeed the romantic spring that never dries for another, as it is greater than a feeling. It is a process that recognizes two hearts in continual desire for each other in laughter, trust, and sharing.

Loving is sharing the world of life with another. It's a people unifier and is never empty or wasted as it opens the gates of happiness. There is no greater thing for two souls to feel they are joined to strengthen each other, to be one with each other in silent unspeakable memories of each other.

I say love is the ultimate test of one's commitment to another. It is an unexplainable passion for another human. A solder commits his or her life for love of country and ideology like freedom and democracy. Love is the best gift we have for each other. Our kindness and love remains our legacy on earth.

This reminds us that love is shared self-giving which end in self-remuneration. Mother Theresa admonished us to spread love everywhere we go and to all children, families and next-door neighbours. Man falls in love partly to avoid solitude and withering away.

It is said that love works wonders and in miracles as it weakens the strong and empowers the weak. A good example can be clearly adduced form story of the case of Delilah and Samson the giant. Love made the great brut Sampson to allow her cut a tuff of his hair, which rendered him instantly weak and lead to his eventual capture.

A fit only love can deliver as armies tried but failed to conquer this monster of a man. Dose love not favour the weak one with passion in this case while at the same time destroying reason? Love dose turn the world going in circles.

Love goes with profound tenderness, which becomes at times almost insupportable. Love is self- sacrificing and responsibility between two. The more a partner gives the more rewarding the relationship becomes heavenly for them.

Love is timeless and removes fear and encourages us to face challenges that would normally frighten others. In short, dear reader, love for me is a free force, a spirit and part of a being needing to be fed by another's' heart to avoid it burning out.

Love is neither a slave to any king nor servant as it develops and dwells equally in both hearts nor follows the laws of nature, which makes the sexes seek love. Again, allow me serenade love by simply saying hurray to priceless love for letting me tick and feel for another heart in this life.

All good things come to an end but true love lives forever. I love you with all my heart said a fiancé to her knight in amour. Hurray to priceless love. It is hoped that this invigorating fairy tale of love left you ruminating on yours years gone by and that you enjoyed reading the work of a novice trying his hand at love story telling for the first time. The tapestry of interwoven true love and fiction was generously bared to readers.

The story makes us mellow and reminiscent our own days and love affairs. It is my hope that the above will let us allow the romantic flame, in us, alight day and night through life. Bless your hearts darling!

Ishfaque Ahmed Dr. Ceesay and Yusuf Mohamed 2009

Manding Medical Centre, Njawara

When God wants to destroy someone, He first made him an unusual dreamer. So Gandhi had his dream of people solving social deference none violently and Martin Luther king, jr. held onto his admirable dream of children of Jews and Gentile, black and whites holding hands and living in harmony spearheading peaceful cause for mankind.

There are the Albert Schweitzer's and mother Theresa's of the world dreamers who spent their lives believing in their dreams for mankind. My dream, since 1956, was the simple goal of providing medical aid to those far and in remote villages.

The villager, who is forced to walk miles on end to seek medical aid for his already dying child, wife or friend, deserves a better health system. Something I saw in 1956 left an indelible mark in my mind and I have since then asked and prayed that God help me bring part if not full solution to the kind of tragedy that was passing right before me.

I was hopelessly unable to give relief except to comfort those involved. In 1956, while on my way to Saba village, I met an anxious father carrying his son and his almost dead pregnant wife on the back of donkey heading for the health center at Kerewan village, another three or more miles from where I met him.

The child was vomiting yellow stuff, he was sweaty, his eyes were reverted backwards and the pregnant lady groaning every time the mule moves. There was some greenish fluid dripping off her lapper. She could barely hold the ropes controlling the donkey.

I went to Kerewan later that evening and asked about the status of that family, only to be told that the boy passed away half a mile to the dispensary and the lady was referred to the central hospital in Banjul but the family had no money to pay for her transportation nor was the River ambulance available as it was undergoing maintenance at the Dockyard.

To cut a long story short, both child and mother died because of lack of medical facilities or modern medical aid to the villager. One or all of those lives could have been saved and remain beneficial to the country than the fate that befell them.

I prayed and grieved with the family for months and redoubled my efforts at school in other to solve such development in future. I committed myself to medicine from that day on and never regretted making such a challenging decision in my lie.Hence, when on the day I was taking the Hippocratic Oath,

I not only swore to uphold all therein but to make sure that God help me not to ever deviate from my commitment and promise to be part of the solution in the health services of the Gambia, to foster health education for the villager, and to complement the existing medical facilities in the Gambia as well as ease the shortage of medical service personnel.

To many, except the dreamer, such ideas lead to failure as they turn to be white elephants. Some friends tease me by flatly promising to rise from their graves on the opening day of such an Alice in wonderland project.Let me make it crystal clear that I had no illusions about what was needed, or to be done and that the building of the hospital would indeed be a lifetime challenge I am fully ready to grapple with. There would be a lot of well-wishers but very few will ever want to join until the opening day ceremonies. Hence, first things first, I met an attorney friend Mr. Ousainou Darboe, a villager like me, on September 24, 1992, and pleaded for his assistance with the legal aspects of setting up a charitable foundation,

Manding Medical center at Njawara village in the provinces for the sole purpose of providing much needed medical aid to the villager. He was very obliging and requested no payment in return for his services. In the mean time I got a board of governors elected while he prepared the memorandum and articles of

association of Manding Medical Centre at Njawara village. Also, I met with the Lower Badibou district chief, Kitabou Singateh, who by the way was my primary school class mate at Kinte Kunda from 1953to 1957, the District Authority, Commissioner and the kerewan Area Council.

All of whom were more than delighted and did all they could under the law to help me set up a grassroots local advisory committee, which was headed by the commissioner, to assist the board and also let the villagers feel being part of the ongoing project.

At my home village, Njawara, a group organized itself and formed a pioneering committee to formally ask the Alkalo (village head/mayor) and the people of Toro Bahen village to donate the earmarked land between it and Njawara for the sole purpose of establishing the Manding Medical Centre on it.

The land issue was partially cleared by the first week of the appeal. And in October 1992, Alkalo Alhaj Omar Koi Bah of Toro Bahen called my brother, Doudu Ceesay, the elders of Toro Bahen and I to officially inform us that the earmarked land of two plots have been donated to me for the sole purpose of erecting a medical center and hospital facility for the villagers of the region and Gambia. We thanked him for his foresight and kindness towards future generations. I went back to my lawyer, Ousainu Darbor who by then had finished all work needed for the registration of Manding Medical Centre. We are forever indebted to Alkalo Omar Koi, residents Arfang Bah, Musa (Nyambi) Bah and Sirimang Bah, and the people of Toro village. Lastly but not least our venerable lawyer Mr. Ousainou Darboe, without whose kindness and legal mind the registration of Manding Medical Centre would have taken longer that it did. I also express profound gratitude to the Hon. Chief of Lower Badibou District, Kitabou Singateh, the commissioner, and the local district authority for their understanding and willingness to contribute positively towards our goal and growth.

I submitted the registration application material to the Attorney General's Chambers at the Justice Department on October 22, 1992 and Manding Medical Centre was officially registered as an incorporated charitable organization under the companies Act, 1959 by the 27th of October 1992.

Manding Medical Centre' certificate of incorporation is number: 224/1992. With the completion of the paper work and registration of the center, I embarked on a blitz of letter writing informing philanthropists and organizations worldwide about Manding Medical Centre and the need for assistance or donations of medications, equipments, medical videos with which to teach our cadre and villagers to become health worker or evangelist, or nurses and to help us build the center.

To complete the establishment process, after the land was officially ours, I wrote to the following letter to the Ministry of Health informing them of the formation of Manding Medical Centre, a self-help health organization at Njawara, Lower Badibou, North Bank Division, The Gambia. Our temporal address was at 5B Ingram Street in Banjul, capital of the Gambia.

Manding Medical Centre
5B Ingram Street
Banjul, The Gambia
March 2, 1993

Permanent Secretary
Ministry of Health
The Quadrangle
Banjul, The Gambia
West Africa

Dear Permanent Secretary,
Re: Application for the establishment of a Medical Centre at Njawara in the North Bank.

We are pleased to bring to attention the setting up of a self-help Health organization in the North Bank Division at Njawara village. The directorates and members of the organization would be more than grateful if the Ministry of Health would allow us establish Manding Medical Centre at Njawara village, Lower Badibou District of the Gambia.

Manding Medical Centre, when fully operational, will provide medical, surgical, gynecological and obstetrics, Pediatrics and other facilities to the villagers. It will also help ease the shortage of medical facilities in that region. Manding Medical Centre will have health education secessions in the villages as an effort to enlighten our youths.

Again, thank you for taking time to consider our application and we certainly look forward to a positive recognition of the need for such a center in the rural sector of the Gambia. I anxiously wait to hear from your office at your convenience. Regards

Yours sincerely

Dr. Alhasan S. Ceesay, MD

Director/Coordinator

Meanwhile the villagers grew more enthused and throngs of them attended our monthly health field trips or clinics. The attendance grew so large that we ended up listing the villages to attend in turn of nine villages per trip. This usually totals to a bit above 1,000 patients at a given visit. I normally go on weekends with three doctors and at times four volunteer doctors along with nurses' aid Mrs. Mbee Sonko and Ida Njie to assist us do the job.

The field trips/clinics start with an announcement by Radio Gambia giving the names of villages expected to attend and at which village health center. The clinic day starts with an early morning breakfast by the team and then a ride to the village health center where we would find the villagers and their sick ones assembled.

Every occasion starts with the offering of prayers and then the various village heads, in attendance help us in organizing the flow of people wanting to be see by one of our team doctors.

In most cases the day goes trouble free but at certain localities the political tension does make it very difficult to have such large groups of people without little arguments. Thanks to the Commissioner (s) for deploying the police or making them available to quell trouble and help us maintain order during these clinics. Commissioner Lamin Koma can tell you how rough things can be at some of these clinic centers. He was trapped in one of these bad moments of people rushing to be in the front line of the queue to see one our doctors. The Ministry of Health finally sent us the following affirmative reply as thus: -

Ministry of Health & Social services
The Quadrangle
Banjul, The Gambia

Ref.P510/289/01 (95)

Dr. Alhasan Ceesay
Manding Medical Centre
5B Ingram Street
Banjul, The Gambia

RE: Application to establish a Medical Centre at Njawara

I acknowledge receipt of your letter of the 2nd March 1993 on the above-mentioned subject. I wish to inform you that this Ministry has no objection to your application to establish Manding Medical Centre at Njawara.

This initiative is in line with our national health policies and we would render our support in our joint efforts to improve the health of the people.

Signed: N. Ceesay
For Permanent Secretary

After several more field trips it was suggested we apply for a none Governmental Organization (NGO) status. It was believed that if we become and NGO, help would come our way quicker.

I went to work on this suggestion and arranged for Tango Secretariat Centre to send one of the United Nations voluntary program officers to come and evaluate our performance relative to the objectives of Manding Medical Centre.

This was accepted and a field trip was set up for September 12 to 22, 1995. Radio Gambia made the announcement well ahead of the time for our arrival and the following was the outcome of that august gathering of September 21 &22, 1995.

Tango Secretariat Trip Report Manding Medical Centre
September 21 – 22, 1995

A field trip to Kerewan at the North Bank Division was organized by the Manding Medical Centre Executive Director Dr. Alhasan S. Ceesay in conjunction with Tango Secretariat Centre to see the organization's activities and meet the members before recommending the organization as a member of Tango.

On September 21, 1995, two meetings were organized in two big centers where members gather to air their views and experience from the organization. Alkalos, chiefs, imams, women, men and youths attended these meetings. The key leadership from five villages in their speeches showed interest and support for the project and organization.

Alkalo of Toro Bahen Omar Koi and chiefs donated the land for the constructing of Manding Medical Centre, the hospital and its ancillaries. The two meeting were highly attended and successful. The Tango (UNV) program officer Mr. Muloshi on behalf of Tango gave a keynote speech on Tango's operations and activities as an umbrella organization and urged members to work hand in hand with the organization in their efforts to develop their villages and North Bank area.

The three meetings with the commissioner during the field trip on our courtesy call were successful and encouraged the executive Director of Manding Medical Centre, Dr. Alhasan Ceesay, to cooperate with the district, especially the commissioner who is one of the advisors in the local committee. The commissioner thanked Tango for making the purpose of the mission clear to him and promised that he will try by all means to cooperate with Tango in the area of Technical advice and institution capacity building. Clinic day was organized on September 22, 1995 at Njawara and 150 people attended and got treatments.

Recommendation

Looking at the caliber of leadership and development activities compared to some NGO tango members in comparison to Manding Medical Centre. The organization needs consideration since they have already activities with a promising future.

Looking at the composition of the Board, they have people with a great vision. They have strong membership and backup at the grassroots levels. The organization has chosen to do what is right at the right time and their concentration in one area is vital and a good starting point. Any success achieved by any organization depended on good leadership and discipline.

Manding Medical Centre has quality leadership and deserves NGO status.

Signed: M. Muloshi
UNV Program Officer

We were delighted by the recommendation made by the United Nations voluntary Program Officer in the Gambia. We redoubled our efforts to contact organizations seeking help worldwide.

In between letters and monthly field trips to different select health centers we were blessed with visits from interested friends and groups or representatives of similar organizations in the globe.I had several telephone calls to Dr. Edward Brown, an official of the World Bank in Washington, D. C. responsible of the bank's health affairs at the time. He was very receptive and had several added discussions with Dentist Melvin George, then Director of Medical and Health Service for the Gambia, on how the bank could help in the financing of the building of Manding Medical Centre.

These talks went on well and Dr. Edward brown gave me his promise and personal commitment to helping the project and that we have to start in a small scale and the building will have to be done in several well planned phases.

A friend Dr. Sidi C. Jammeh promised help to keep the momentum at the World Bank alive by consulting with and constantly reminding Dr. Brown the need to help our Manding Medical Centre's project.

Among our guest were a couple from Colchester, Essex, UK, Lorna V. Robinson and husband Keith Robinson were very impressed by our project and enthusiasm of the ordinary villagers about Manding Medical Centre.

They fell in love with the idea and objectives of the self-help health organization and promised to help as much as they could. We had by this time submitted application for NGO status and ACCNO Secretary replied thus:

ACCNO Secretariat
Dept. of Community Development
13 Mariner Parade
Babjul, The Gambia
September 12, 1994

Ref.CD/ACCNO/Vol3/ (183)

Dr. Alhasan S. Ceesay
Director/Coordinator
Manding Medical Centre
P. O. Box 640
Banjul, The Gambia

Dear Sir,

RE: application for an NGO status within the ACCNO framework

Please find enclosed a self-explanatory letter from the Ministry for local government and lands concerning the approval of your application for NGO status.

ACCCNO Secretariat congratulates your organization for successfully completing the registration process and wishes you a fruitful relationship in the field of development.

Thank you for your cooperation

Yours Faithfully
Musu Ngujo
For: ACCNO desk Officer
Cc: file & R/File

Replies from our worldwide appeal letters did not pour in money nor did these materialized beyond promises to help in due course. Hence, I decided to open up a pharmacy at my expense at my residence in the Bundung area of Serekunda using the proceeds from its sales to finance the health field trips and activities of the organization. This meant spending an extra three to fours at the pharmacy daily after eight hours at the RVH before rejoining my family. All drugs used for the treatment of patients at our field trip clinics were purchased from sales I made at the Bundung Pharmacy. A local agency, known as IBAS, lent me D8000, interest free, which was used in buying drugs and paying for transportation for the project's activities.

The loan was completely repaid well ahead of the allowed sixteen months period given by IBAS. We are obliged and grateful to Aja Ndey Oley Jobe and management of IBAS for their kindness to assist us at the time.

Just when things were about to be financially complete for us to start the first phase of building the various sections of the hospital, came the unexpected coup d'etat of July 22, 1994. The reaction from would be our donors and supporters or sponsors were swift and equally unexpected.

All those who were considering giving the project a chance sited likelihood of sudden national unrest and instability as reasons for their withdrawal of promised aid and participation while some suggested my waiting until after the transition phase of the coup d'etat before they would reconsider reopening our files with them.

Again it resorted to case of the chicken the egg, which came first as no one, knew when the transition will end and we kept our fingers crossed hoping that daylight will be ours in not far distance.

It was a severe blow to our hope and for getting the type of interest and support that was engendered for Manding Medical Centre would be difficult to match after such crisis that occurred in the Gambia.

Many were acting in conjunction with their governments, which were not sure of what the future under military rule would be for the Gambia. All prospective and possible international sources earmarked for Manding Medical Centre were either frozen or evaporated into thin air with the coup leaving me floating in the middle of the ocean of despair without a life jacket except God's merciful hands. I knew the villagers would grow restless if nothing happens in the direction of building the center.

I called an emergency general meeting with members from most of the villages and told them of the new challenge and development and this information not only fell on deaf ears but left their spirits dampened.Interest waxed and waned at some quarters but I kept on trying my best not to be despondent like the others have shown.

I kept the organization alive under very limited funds raised from the pharmacy at Bundung until my trip to the UK in January 2000. Before leaving the Gambia, the Commissioner for north Bank Division and chairman of the local advisory committee for Manding Medical Centre, Mr. Lamin Koma, gave me the following letter to assist me in my fund raising drive while in England and possible other European countries. It read thus:

The Commissioner
Kerewan Village
North Bank Division
The Gambia, West Africa

June 15, 1998

To whom it may concern

I hereby write to testify and confirm that Manding Medical Centre is a self-help health project situated at Njawara village, North Bank Division. As the Commissioner of this division I was elected as the Chairman of the local advisory Committee of the Manding Medical Centre.

As I am concerned, I am aware of this self-help project since it took off the ground, by the able hands of Dr. Alhasan S. Ceesay, a born citizen of Njawara village. The purpose of the establishing of such a medical centre is to provide medical attention/care to all Gambians irrespective of religion, tribe, nationality or gender and age within the country and sub-region.

It is in these regards that this office writes to seek for your assistance in providing support in cash/kind to make this medical center a reality. I look forward to your continued support and cooperation.

  Signed: V. Baldeh
  For Commissioner
  North Bank Division

The new millennium started with good omen for Manding Medical Centre. I have been invited to go to Europe and America on a found raising trip for the center but could not because of my commitment with the Royal Victoria Hospital (RVH).

I needed a longer vacation period to be able to travel and keep my job at the sane time. Above all my family needed the monetary support, which would fade away if I lost the post at the RVH. Hence, to my delight and greatest timely occurrence I heard from my long-standing friend in Colchester, Mrs. Lorna V. Robinson, inviting my wife and I to come to the UK to attend the wedding of their younger daughter on January 9th, 2000. Coincidentally, I had just started my annual leave, which was to finish on the 26th of January 2000.

The excitement mounted when we received a fax from the visa officer at the British High Commission in the Gambia requesting that we report to the visa processing office with our passports on Tuesday 8.30 am January 4th, 2000 for processing of our visas for our pending travels to the UK. This took me by surprise because of the casual way we had discussed the possibility of such a trip.

So when we got the telephone call followed by the said fax from the visa section I was caught off guard and had to rush through all the preparations for my wife and I to travel to UK without a second thought on whether adequate arrangements were being made for my eventual pursuit of a postgraduate degree (MRCP) in internal medicine.

Hind side has it that I needed to discuss this aspect with the visa councilor and request for eventual student visa status or leave to remain until my completion of the post graduate degree I wanted to pursue. God's ways and timing are best for every occasion.

I was yearning to get a way out of the financial limbo the center ran into since the change of government in the Gambia. Now that opportunity was suddenly thrown on my laps by Lorna Robinson's open-ended invitation for my wife and to attend their daughter's wedding ceremony in the UK.

Interested donors started being weary about Military rule and possible restlessness that may ensue. Hence, Manding Medical Centre literally lost all its prospective overseas support as well as sponsors most of who had cold feet after the July coup d'etat of 2004.

I ended up running the center from my meager salary of D1500 or seventy-five pounds sterling per month and of literally hard labour with long hours at a time. The other source was from what little I could make from sales at the Bundung pharmacy.

To cut a long story short we were granted visas to travel to the UK. We left the Gambia on the 6th of January 2000 on a new footing and challenge to bring back some life into Manding Medical center while in England. I got on the ball as soon as the wedding ceremony was over. I obtained a three–year study leave from the Management Board of the Royal Victoria Hospital in Banjul. This gave me all the time I needed to try to rekindle interest in the center and thereby inject into Manding Medical center cash flow it needed to help us meet or our targeted goal and objective for the farming community in the North Bank Division of the Gambia.

It was more like a miracle entering this new concrete and direct ways. Help from my host Lorna Robinson of Colchester, Essex, UK further anointed my hands. Lorna and I wrote several letters to various places, including celebrities and organizations, most of who replied in the negative because of perception they had about the political climate in Gambia since the coup d'etat of July 22nd 1994. Nonetheless some hinted being interested at a later date, meaning when the solders return to camp.

A few donated small amounts plus hospital items. By now it became clear that we have to counter the perception most, on this side of the isles feel or had about the Gambia at the time. This dreadful start did not alarm me much for I am fully aware of the wrong information about the average African in the village, who like most, is just a decent human being trying to earn an honest living for himself, family and community.

Villagers are least interested in all the political gimmickry shrouding and clothing their lives. I do not at all blame the rest of world for getting sick and tired of helping and not seeing any tangible good come out of it and worse some African politicians and regimes show no interest in helping move the African people onto better and modern rewarding modalities of life.

They offer more lip service than opening avenues for progress. How many knew that the Ethiopian starvation was politically orchestrated by the then Mangestu regime? Genocide regime and the heartlessness of some African politicians made me feel sick.

To remove any possible skeptics regarding Manding Medical Centre and its objectives we decided to have it registered as a charitable organization in the UK under the name of Colchester Friends of Manding charitable trust. The Robinson knew a solicitor who would be so kind to help us with the legal aspect of the registration process with UK charity Commission.

They spoke to Mr. Bruce Ballard of the Birkett long Solicitors to come to our aid. This kind gentleman, like my lawyer friend, Mr. Ousainou Darboe, gladly agreed to help and sent us a draft of the Trust deed.

After a series of changes were made on the draft he forwarded our request to be registered in the UK as a charitable organization helping its twin partner or parent group, Manding Medical Centre at Njawara village in the Gambia, West Africa. Meanwhile, we concentrated our activities through media campaign effort to call attention to existence of Friends of Manding and their desire in building a hospital for Manding Medical Centre at Njawara, the Gambia.

Again we ran into a very gentle heart in the person of Miss Helen Anderson of Colchester who was the Community website editor for Essex County. She went head over heels regarding the idea of helping others so far away when approached by Lorna Robinson.

Helen thought the idea wonderful and at the same time helped us have our own website and also had an article published by the Evening Gazette which had a large reader circulation.

In the same vein I got the interest of Dr. Linda Mahon-Daly, Dr. Peter Wilson, Dr. Laurel Spooner, Dr. Richard Spooner, Dr. Philip Murray, Dr. Barbara Murray, Dr. Fredric Payne, who by the way was our Medical superintendent under who I worked at the RVH during the later part of colonial Gambia, along with many surgeries in the Colchester area.

These were my Good Samaritans of the day who worked acidulously to make Manding Medical Centre become a reality for the villagers in the Gambia. Dr. Linda Mahon-Daly helped distribute letters about Manding Medical Centre to nearly all her colleagues in the Colchester Borough and so did Dr. Laurel Spooner. Bless their hearts for kindness and job well done.

The news article published by the Evening Gazette brought us another very helpful and kind person, Mr. Malkait singh who is an ophthalmologist and had made several trips to the Gambia before knowing about the Friends of Manding. He was delighted to join Neville Thompson, Connie Thompson, Lorna Robinson, Keith Robinson, Loenard Thompson, Mark Naylor, Barbara Philips and others as pioneering members of Friends of Manding. Mr. Malkait Singh and I grew to be very good friends and he had since given me lots of personal monetary help to cater for my exams and family back in the Gambia. I am very grateful for interest and kindness, and concern he showed about my family. A few months after the formation of Friends of Manding, Dr. Laurel Spooner spent a week in the Gambia vacationing and doing some fact finding about the center.

During which time she visited Manding Medical Centre at Njawara in the North Bank Division. The villagers were happy to meet her and thanked her about good work being done in Colchester regarding Manding Medical Centre. Everyone was happy about the news that people in the UK were poised to assist Manding Medical Centre go forward in its drive to provide medical aid to villagers. A meeting of member of the Friends of Manding was scheduled for the first week of February 2001.Mean while our solicitor continued pressing for registration of Friends of Manding, which is the arm and Manding Medical Centre's Colchester branch support group, as charity in the UK. Dr. Laurel Spooner suggested we start with small-scale form of the center and then gradually expand as funds become available. This consideration would be studied in full and deliberated upon by the committee during the forthcoming February meeting.

What Is Manding Medical Centre?

Manding Medical Centre located at Njawara village in the North Bank of Gambia (NBD), West Africa is a self-help village health organization founded by Dr. Alhasan S. Ceesay.(NBD), West Africa. Its objective is to provide medical service to the villagers by providing efficient and affordable medical aid to all people in and around the Gambia, especially the rural sector.

We are dedicated to relieving suffering and ensure effective treatment for villagers and all attending Manding Medical Centre at Njawara, NBD.

Established

The Manding Medical Centre is founded by Dr. Alhasan Sisawo Ceesay, a native of Njawara village in 1992 because of the sheer shortage of medical service to the region and the preponderance of premature deaths by children from Malaria, malnutrition, diarrhea, and worm infestations.

These maladies account for almost 25% of Gambian children's death before the ripeful age of 5 years. The Gambia Ministry of Health officially recognized the Centre in 1995 and prior to which it became a None Governmental Organization (NGO) on September 12th, 1994.

Mission Statement

Suffering in another human being is a call to the rest of us to stand in fellowship. It requires us to be there and it is a mystery, which demands the spirit of caring, sharing and our presence. Our duty as healthcare professionals is providing medical care, which is a fundamental right of all human beings. This village health organization is dedicated to providing medical aid to the rural sector and farming community in the Gambia. It will compliment the health service in the Gambia in addition it will promote preventive medicine in the hinterland of the Gambia.

Membership

Well over twenty thousand villagers, comprising of farmers, village heads, chiefs, the Kerewan Area Council, commissioners and local District Authority are now fully active enthusiastic members of Manding Medical Centre. All are welcomed to join the endeavors of the center. People from the rest of the globe are more than welcomed to participate or share with us our dream in bring much needed medical service to people in desperate state because of lack of medical facilities.

Activity

Manding Medical Centre tries to alleviate some of the above mentioned health problems and situations by having bimonthly health field trip/clinic to villages teaching them about health, preventive medicine and hygiene that would help reduce the number infected and the vectors responsible for these diseases.

We encourage antenatal and postnatal attendance of clinics by mothers and we treat the sick amongst them with minimum charge to not so elderly and pregnant young ladies. The service is free to children, the very elderly, and the indigent needing emergency treatment. The rest pay amounts well below tat in private practice. Money accrued is subsequently used to buy drugs with which to treat the patients and for other projects of the center. When in cession the center treats well more than 1000 patients per field trip to the villages. We provide free information and advisory service on aids and sexually transmitted diseases (STDs) to the young, all patients, their relatives and friends. We also plan to have a Nursing School in due course to augment not only staff but also the government health centers when the need assistance.

Our Immediate Goal and Appeal

The villagers are very enthused about the center and Toro Bahen village, next to Njawara village, has donated two plots of land for the building of the center and its ancillary units, which is now leased to Manding medical center for ninety-nine years.
More than 2000 children die tragically from malaria and other childhood ailments stated above for shortage of health services. We are eager to start building the children' and maternity wings of the proposed Gambia General Hospital at Manding Medical Centr and do need raise the required 900,000 pounds sterling to accomplish our goal.
10 bags of cement cost thirty pounds sterling or $60 (sixty us dollars). Also we would be most grateful if we could be assisted with medicines and equipment to facilitate our work. Hence we implore you to kindly support our yearning to build the children' and maternity wings of Manding Medical Centre.

We are dedicated to providing medical aid to the villager, especially children. We are investors in people and you are invited to join the endeavors of Manding Medical Centre at Njawara village, the Gambia, West Africa. Help us make a difference and beacon of hope for the villagers. Please give generously. Today's hope can be tomorrow's reality. We want to contribute positively towards the health services of the Gambia, and with this center in place it will create greater health awareness and privation by the villagers.

Cash contributions of any amount should be sent in the name of Manding Medical Centre, to the Friends of Manding charitable Trust, 82 Finchingfield Way, Blackheath, Colchester, Essex, CO2 OAU, and England.It is vital to be certain that Dr. Alhasan S. Ceesay is informed of your contribution via email thus: alhasanceesay@hotmail.com. Your kindness and humane consideration to help save lives will always be deeply appreciated and grateful for by the villagers, the Gambia and I.

Overseases links

The Friends of Manding in Colchester, Essex County is formed by local group of residents, doctors, and nurses who regularly visited the Gambia and are in support of Manding Medical Centre. Manding medical center through the auspices of the Friends of Manding recently received recognition and registration by the UK Charity Commission.

They serve as support and our liaison in the Europe Union. The Friends of Manding in behalf of Manding Medical Centre at Njawara has been entered in the central Register of charities with effect from August 21, 2001; the registration number is 1088136 for England and Wales. Also, a similar charitable trust, the Alpena Friends of Manding Charitable Trust of Michigan, USA, has been established in Alpena, Michigan in June 2006. It's headed by Dr. Avery Aten a resident physician chairman of the Women and newborn of the Alpena region Community Health along with the medical community of Alpena.

Dr. Alhasan Ceesay, Mohamed Sheriff Azaan UK 2007

Manding Med. Centre Milestones

Manding Medical Centre has been in my mind's drawing board since the early 1950s but it took off in earnest when I returned to the Gambia, after graduating from medical school in 1992. The Centre is registered as a charity with the Attorney general's Office, Department of Justice, Banjul, The Gambia, since 1993.
The Gambia Ministry of Health also recognized it in the same year.Toro Bahen village, Lower Badibou, NBD, Gambia, donated two huge plots of land for the location of the center in 1993. Our none governmental (NGO) status was approved in 1994. On September 21, 1995 Tango Secretariat sent a United Nations voluntary program Officer,
Mr. Muloshi on field trip to evaluate the organizational and extent of support for Manding Medical Centre at Njawara village. Mr. Muloshi's recommendation after two days field trip to the region stated thus; "Looking at the caliber of leadership and development activities to some NGO Tango members in comparison to Manding Medical Centre, the organization need consideration since they have already activities with a promising future.
Looking at composition of the Board, they have people with a vision.They have strong membership and backup at grass root levels. The organization has chosen to what is right at the right time and their concentration in one area is vital and good starting point.
Any success achieved by any group or organization depends on good leadership and discipline. Manding Medical Centre has high quality leadership and deserves NGO status."

It was not until my travels to the UK in 2000 that the Friends of Manding Charitable Trust was formed and registered as charity in England and Wales by the UK Charity Commission. Friends of Manding is the extended arm of Manding Medical Centre at Njawara, The Gambia. They serve as our liaison in the UK and the European Union. Please browse on our website thus: friendsofmandinggambimed.btck.co.uk, to learn more or for further information about our work and organization. We are still on fund raising activities to earn enough to enable us build the children' and maternity units of the hospital at Manding Medical Centre at Njawara.

In May 2005, 11 American students and their instructor Mr. Thomas Ray visited Manding Medical Centre at Njawara. Additionally, input from has now resulted in Alpena City, Michigan, USA, twining by proclamation with Njawara and Kinte kunda villages in Gambia respectively on the 5th of December 2005.

In June 2006, Dr. Avery Aten, Chairman of the Women and Newborn of Alpena Region Health Community along with the medical community of Alpena commenced processing application for a charitable Trust to be named Alpena friends of Manding Charitable Trust, Michigan, USA.

This will soon be finalized and up and running to help Dr. Alhasan Ceesay in the provision of medicine and educational assistance to schools in the Lower Badibou district, the Gambia, West Africa. In August 2008, Dr. Alhasan Ceesay and the Badibou Cultural Dance Troupe will visit Alpena and other cities in Michigan for fund raising drive to enable the building of the Manding

Medical Centre children and maternity units at Njawara village. Dr. Richard Bates, an Obynge, and a number of medical professionals involved in obstetrics and gynecology at Alpena, Michigan joined Manding Medical Centre's crusade on 17/o8/07.

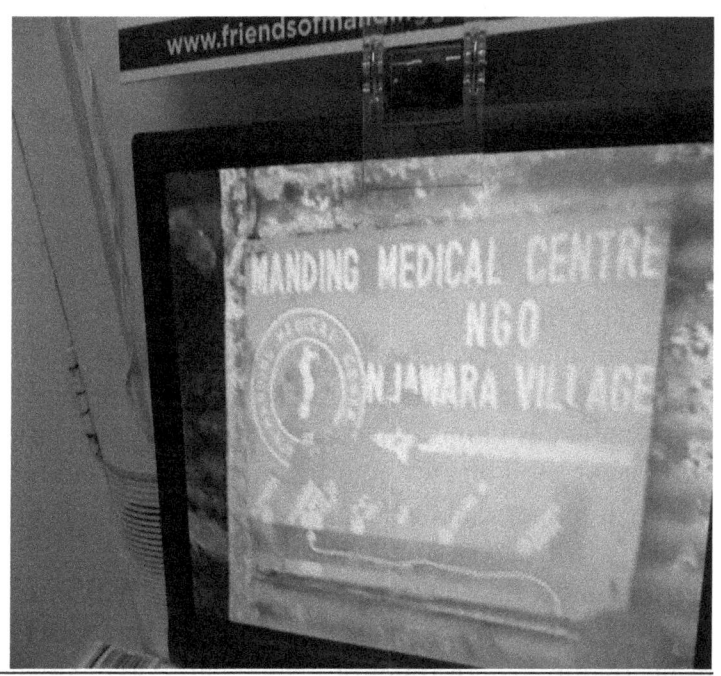

An Appeal for Help from the International Community

Dear Readers,

The above information about Manding Medical Centre is included in this work only hoping that it will help spread the word more extensively and draw awareness to a greater community of people and readers of my work.

It is my belief that lots of good people out there may want to participate or give to the cause and goal of the center should they be aware of its existents for the villagers.

Hence, I am appealing for help and participatory support from all able to extend their hearts to make this much needed medical endeavor to come to fruition for the rural sector of the Gambia. Who knows you might even end up coming to bask in our beautiful seasides and relish Gambian generosity.

Music for me is reaching out to help others and my patients are yearning for your kind participation and donation in cash/kind. Thanks a million for considering our appeal. God blesses your heart(s). I write with belief that by it money can be generated to provide a much needed medical service to the rural sector.

Writing about the Manding Medical Centre may course some Good Samaritan and any wanting to leave foot prints on the sand of time for a good cause to come to our assistance to help us meet the goals of the center at Njawara village, the Gambia, West Africa.

My head, heart and soul are devoted to my family, the Gambia and Manding Medical Centre. It is not a God given calling but a mere conviction that our rural folks deserve better health service than currently available and hence human calling to want to contribute positively to bring resolution of some of our rural health service inadequacies. I never had an angel come down to me nor have I ever heard the voices of God saying, "Ceesay, you must do so and so" as many mocked Manding Medical Centre emanated from sheer conviction that it is a dutiful way of doing the right thing for curbing premature deaths of children before reaching 5 years of life from malaria, water born diseases, and warm infestations; and in the same vein providing both pre and postnatal care to the pregnant.

Hence, portions of proceeds of sales in all my work go to help meet the center's operational costs and in providing scholarship to indigent indigenous rural candidates wishing to read for a medical degree or agriculture and in due course return to serve rural Gambia.

I write to draw attention of the International community to Manding Medical Centre at Njawara and also in believing that my life's experience could be inspirational to the despondent and also to make certain that this villager will continue to do all he could to bring medical relief to rural Gambia.

We lost Lorna Robinson, Secretary of Friends of Manding at Colchester and good right hand who believed and was dedicated to the cause of Manding Medical Centre. Thank you for purchasing this work and hence for participating in our dream of providing much needed modern medical service to the often-neglected villagers of hinterland Africa.

A Tribute to Lorna V. Robinson

Tribute to Lorna V. Robinson

As friends and family bit farewell to a unique, caring, sharing and rare angel of mercy, allow me share a snippet or bird's eye view about Lorna Valerie Robinson. Mrs. Lorna Robinson and I met through her job as a general nurse at the then Essex County General Hospital in Colchester in 1990, when I was a trainee doctor at the Essex County hospital.

She and husband became my friends and they visit my family in Gambia annually. In my village Lorna became the modern Pipe Piper of Hamlin town as children with bright eyes swamp her from all sides. One could hear chorus of Auntie Lorna is here. Welcome to Gambia, Auntie Lorna. The Robinson's became my England and together we set to catch a dream of providing medical aid and service to Gambian villagers in the North Bank Region.

Keith, Dr. Ceesay, late Lorna Robinson

Lorna and I have since 2000 worked acidulously to make the coveted dream of providing medical service come to fruition for the villagers. It was Lorna Robinson's joint efforts with, nurses, doctors Laura Spooner, Richard Spooner, Barbara Murray, Philip Murray, Linda Malhon-Daly, and Malkait Singh along with Colchester residents Connie Thompson, Neville Thompson and Keith Robinson which led to the formation of the Colchester Friends of Manding Charitable Trust, which, with help of solicitors was registered in England and Wales as a charity by the UK Charity Commission in August 2001 and our charity number is 1088136.

The Colchester Friends of Manding Charitable Trust serves as extension of Manding Medical Centre at Njawara and doubles as our liaison in the European Community. Lorna spent countless weekends either selling materials; such as toys, cloths, coats and anything she could lay her hands on as long as she believes it will generate money for the building of the children and maternity units of the Manding Medical Centre at Njawara in Gambia.

She continued to promote the course of the above by holding weekend bazaars at different places in Colchester and with ladies at Bingos. Influence of this Good Samaritan group in Colchester reverberated and led to the formation of a similar charity group in America, with Dr. Avery Aten heading that effort.

Through his leadership emanated the Alpena friends of Manding Charitable Trust in Michigan, USA, and it was approved in 2005.All of which came by because Lorna, the lady of mercy, would not rest while the indigent goes without the most basic things in life.

Lorna was one willing and delighted to help others. She used to say, "In life we most extend our hearts to others and with compassion reach the needy." For my villagers she was hope and knowledge that someone so far away, whom they have never met, cared about them.

Lorna was concerned that millions suffer needlessly for not having means of proper healthcare, clean and safe water, food, and good shelter etc. She more than any wanted to help the villagers from descending into a downward spiral of deepening healthcare deprivation.

When am in low spirit she would quote Albert Schweitzer, "Any who proposes to do good must not expect people to move stone away from his path but most accept his lot if even a few more are placed on his way". It was this unique caring angel the villagers and I lost on the third of March 2010.

Loosing Lorna V. Robinson left feeling having lost one the best person, outside of my family, I ever known. She was a kind soul of unswerving determination to share the little she had with others less fortunate needing help. Lorna stood by my cause in thick and thin moments of my stay in the UK, when most had given up on my mission for the villagers and me.

The provision of medical care to the rural sector in Gambia is more than a responsibility; it is a sacred duty and trust to me. It is a call I have dedicated my life and work on archiving it for as long as it may take to accomplish. I will never let my villagers or the memory of Lorna V. Robinson down because of trepidations and like her I believe in looking to the well being of the less fortunate.

One cares on trying, upon reflecting on all the children and villagers who sincerely need this healthcare. Hence, I repeat, Lorna Robinson, no trepidation will stop or hold me back. Finally, my family, villagers, in fact the entire Gambia and I miss and deeply mown her premature and untimely departure from mother earth.

May she rest in eternal peace with her maker and may we the living without fail or fear able to follow her high and shining examples of the indefatigable, Good Samaritan she was in life. I hope you will join me to keep goals of Manding Medical Centre and Lorna's memory and legacy alive for others to copy.

Lorna, thanks for sharing your life with us and for loving us. A million thanks and goodbye for now!

Signed: Dr. Alhasan S. Ceesay, MD,
Founder/co-ordinator
Manding Medical Centre
Njawara village, Lower Badibou, NBR,
The Gambia, West Africa.

Email: *alhasanceesay@hotmail.com*

My Samaritan Men of Good Will

Every successful person had Samaritan angels who offered their shoulders for him or her to stand on and see further than most. Compiled herein are my Samaritan men of goodwill. Hence, I beg leave to indulge in a bit of sentimentality about a few rare human angels who played major part in today's success and help for my villagers. Believe me their moulds, as you will soon find, are beyond those of simple people.

These men help me reach today's pedestal. In medicine for the villager, I profiled ladies who championed my cause. Now, bear with me for just a few lines on the Samaritan men of goodwill. They like the previously mentioned ladies all not only believe in my dream and objective for the villager but also gave all they could to help make that dream come to fruition.

These men gave unparalleled needed help and friendship to me when I was distressed and in utter despair and darkness. Some even shed a few tears with me because the pain and set back certain roadblocks caused my goal. One of these was the day I received GMC' e-mail of the 17th June 2008 recanting recognition of my primary medical qualification based on frivolous website enter.

Hell brewed and peculated to its hottest temperatures, as it took time to unravel the misunderstanding, before GMC rectified the error. However, with your indulgence let us start from the beginning of the geneses. It was with God' anointing hand in conjunction with Sisawo Bajo Ceesay, alias Sisawo Salah that my twin partner I landed on this Garden of Eden.

Father gave us love and good guidance throughout his life with us. He and I had deferent perception about western Education and culture but we reconciled after my completing primary school at Kinte Kunda. My father's experience from the hands of colonials made him never to entertain idea of his progeny deviating from the farmers' mold.

Nor would he allow me pursue Western Education and ideology, which at the time was alien to my father and his peers. He once told me: Son, my wish for you is to be a hard working good farmer and not indulge in the quagmire and sleaze world of spin-doctors. I do not want you tinkering with ideology that would infuse into you wrong philosophies about life and God.

My father came from a different generation with totally different perceptions about invaders ruling them. Let us for a moment step into their shoes to find out why the resistance for their progeny to attend school.

In my father's days men believed in God, the sanctity of life and peaceful coexistence of the communities they lived. About the invading longhaired men he called devils, father said: "Son the way these men, meaning the colonialist, took over our countries can only be the work of the devil.

They came from the blue sea and seized our land and minerals, and remaining on the best parts while leaving us the worst places to farm and for our animals to grace. To pour oil on fire they requested that we change our religions and ways to their dark and indiscipline life styles.

To top up, our people were forced to live under laws promulgated by the invaders on top of which we must pay to learn their languages while they make systemic concerted efforts to distorted and destroy everything that was dear to us. They massacred, disgraced, and dethroned all our kings and chiefs.

These shameful acts were reinforced with policies of divide and rule by pitting tribe against tribe and even bribing those bad elements willing to do their dirty work. Wages paid to workers were not worth the coin they were minted on.

They made certain no organization, political or professional civil service existed in our countries".

He said, "They filled the jails with those of us who refused to be indoctrinated or accept the supremacy of the foreign invaders.

So Son, because of kindheartedness and gentled nature of the African our ways are undermined and thrown out by invaders who replaced it with greed, unkindness, spin-doctoring, and lack of respect for man and nature. He concluded by saying, these are just a few reasons why I would not let my blood attend school".

The above is a pinhole view of father's radicalism and patriotic views. He did recap late later in his old age and finally gave full blessings to my efforts and future goals. He passed away peacefully to his maker in 1991 while I was a trainee doctor doing my clinical clerkship rotation at Colchester General Hospital in Colchester, Essex County, England.

Notices no matter how simple were just bundles of scribbles on worthless paper to the farmer. The illiterates who cannot decipher the prints are cheated of their rights and land.

I was not going to be among those who cannot decipher the print and hence found my way to Kinte Kunda Primary School where I met with the head Master, Mr. Louis Albert Bouvier, who hails from Banjul, our capital city.

This benevolent teacher was my first real contact with Western Education and we gelled instantly and became inseparable He allowed me to stay at his home and treated me as his own son. He was kind and firm and wasted no time teaching me about life and on how to compete without strangulating the competitor.

He told me repeatedly that competition was a healthy fund and stressed that one must be honest and have integrity and tolerance in life. He counseled hard work at everything one did. Above all, it was incumbent on me to have faith and to serve God daily, if not more but never less. Also he allowed me all the freedom a growing child needed without pampering me.

He did lay certain straightforward and simple rules for me. I was to study at a designated time, return home in time whenever I went into town, unless given an extension by him, and to be in bed by 10:00 pm, with lights off whether sleepy or not. He insisted that I perform my five daily prayers as expected of my religion even though he was devoured Catholic.

Mr. Bouvier would only help with my homework when he felt that I have done my best at it and that I was not trying to have him do the work. Otherwise, he would let me go and make a fool of myself before the class before I deserve his coveted help. Hash you think but this strict beginning or treatment, as you would call it, made me do well at school and do things with confidence independently at very tender age.

I remain profoundly grateful to Mr.Louis Albert Bouvier for being educational springboard, for being a sincere and true friend and mentor. Something said by Francis Farmer summed up the relationship between L. A. Bouvier and me. She said, "To have a good friend is the purest of all God' gifts, for it is a love that has no exchange of payments. It is not inherited, as with family.

It is not compelling, as with a child. And it has no means of physical pleasures, as with a mate. It is, therefore, an indescribable bond that brings with it a far deeper devotion than others". Mr. L. A Bouvier continued to help and mold my academic life until when I started Armitage School in 1957. Leaving a friend like Mr. Bouvier was difficult and emotional for both of us.

We have become one and are now to say farewell and perhaps separate forever. He prepared me well but like any parent or true friend he worried about the difficulties that lay ahead. I just wished they had transferred him with me to Armitage.

On the day I boarded the land rover to Armitage tears rundown Mr. Bouvier's cheeks and mother turned her head away to hide her own. L. A. Bouvier was my best friend, after the loss of my twin brother, fate had it that I was now about to be far away from all I knew and loved. Mr. L. A. Bouvier kept cautioning me to, "keep your head up and do your school works.

You have never been a failure, and even if such a sad experience occurs, keep trying over and over to overcome it. We send you to Armitage with prayers, pride and above all with our deepest love. May God keep you in good health. Goodbye, Mr. Ceesay." It was very moving for this was the first time he addressed me as Mr. Ceesay.

We boarded the Land Rover and as it started to move Bouvier followed for some distance exhorting me not to fear to ask for help when need arose. He kept saying he would gladly help or would ask my parents to pitch in whenever possible. Mr. L. A. Bouvier and I kept in touch despite the distance poor mail service of those days. The link continued while I was in the USA.

I lost my friend in a motorcar accident, six year before returning from America in 1974. His vehicle is said to have ran off the road went over a hill. Another part of me went with him. The evil that men do lives after them and the good is interred with their bodies.

Well rest assured that L. A. Bouvier's good deeds did remain alive and intact on earth. At Armitage it was a newly qualified teaches from Kaur, Mr. Keko B. A. Manneh, who then doubled as our class' English and Mathematics teacher that filled in gap left by my leaving L. A. Bouvier at Kinte Kunda.

He was soft-spoken Chaucerian, a nickname we gave him because he crammed the entire work of Chaucer. He too loved me and was a good guide at Arbitrage. I am grateful for encouragement and help he gave and for really being there when I needed an honest person to open up to about difficulty or academic aspiration.

I left for New York on the 24 August 1967 and arrived at Alpena Michigan 1:30 Am on the 25 August 1967. Mr. Henry V. Vali, a counselor and foreign student advisor at Alpena Community College, was at the bus station to pick me. After the formality of welcoming me to Alpena he drove me to 251 Washington Avenue the home of Mr. Howard Riggs where it had been agreed I stay until start of the semester in September before moving to Russell

Wilson Hall at the Alpena Community College campus. Not surprising Mr. Vali and I became friends and remained so ever since. Mr. Howard Riggs and family welcomed me home as late as it was on that glorious day when I set foot in Michigan.

They were all delighted to have me in their lovely home and they gave me princely meal to nourish my body and milk to quench my thirst. Howard owned Ice-Cream Pallor down Town. He was very modest, delightful man and above all a very generous person.

Soon Mr. and Mrs. Riggs became mom and dad throughout my American stay for their overwhelmingly kind people deserving such salutation from a poor villager. Howard's warmth and generosity to other made his family unique company to foreign students coming to Alpena.

The Riggs were the ideal Americans to me. They were average working family who readily shared the little bit God gave them with others less fortunate. I remained grateful to these kind-hearted friends. Mr. Vali and Mr. Thomas Rither, Director of Foreign students at ACC, and I met several time to discuss my financial nightmare.

Mr.Ritter too concerned that the college might Face INS censure is he allowed my staying without a sponsor or means of paying the tution fees and catter for myself.

He was adamant and made it very clear to me that failure to get help for the first semester will leave him with no other option but to advise the immigration to consider deporting proceedings against me. He gave a week ultimatum for me to sort things out before our next meeting 18 September 1967. Copies of letters from my sponsor Mr. Isdor Gold never move or evoke sympathy from him as he epidermises a true inelastic bureaucrat. Mr. Henry V. Vali convinced Mr. Thomas Ritter to hold on while get in touch with some residents about my case. He was on the telephone to different would be possible sympathizers to my cause.

Most of who agreed to contribute toward the cost of my first semester at Alpena Community College. Vali also spoke to the president of the college in my behalf to prevent Mr. Ritter from hastily and unilaterally contacting the INS for frivolous fears in his head.

My plight soon became a house whole affair and many residents pitched in to help resolve the case.Mr. Vali, Mrs. Glennie spearheaded the appeal and very soon it snowballed letting me start my first semester at Alpena Community College, in Alpena, Michigan. Fr. John miller at St. Bernard Rectory in Alpena not only lent me $250 but evangelized my state in every sermon for three weeks netting me much needed financial help.

God bless his heart. He left Alpena before my transfer to Olivet College in Olivet Michigan in 1979. Judge Philip Glennie was head of the 26th circuit Court of Michigan at the time. His wife, Mrs. Viola Gennie, was professor of foreign language at Alpena Community College. Both not only contributed substantial amounts towards my tuition but also became my adopted parents in Alpena.

They continued to link with me like wise support my goal until their return to heaven in the late nineties. I remember these friends with joy mingled with sadness that they are not here to share reward they showed but also I remember them with intense gratitude for role and kindness shown me while a student at Alpena Community College, Alpena, Michigan, USA.

In another vein Alpena Community College gave me part time job at the Library and a summer job at the Salmon Experimental Fish hatchery. Thanks to grand efforts of Mr. Henry V. Vali and residents of Alpena I was able to overcome the financial crisis of my first semester at the college.

Members of the Gambia Support Network, Manchester

L – R: Dr. A. Ceesay, Prof. Sul Nyang, Mr. Cloyd Ramsey
And Prof. Francis Conti

I met Mr. Cloyd Ramsey while seeking a summer job at the Medical Arts Clinic in Alpena. He was then manager of the unit at the time. Upon hearing my plight he promised to see what he could do even though the clinic itself had no jobs openings for that summer. I left him impressed and very moved by what he heard.

He too became an integral part of my time and sojourner in America than any through contributions and loans he took from the Alpena bank in my behalf to support my studies throughout my stay in the USA and short stay in Liberia, West Africa.

It was through kindness of Mr. Ramsey and his sponsorship that enabled Michigan Technological University at Houghton to accept me does a Masters program in Biological Sciences from 1971 to 1973.

It was Mr. Cloyd Ramsey who came to my rescuer when things went very bad and unbearable and practically unsafe for me after the military coup d'état against William Tolbert' administration of Liberia in 1981.

He provided a round trip Air ticket to the USA and supporting it with invitation for me as their guest at Sandusky, Michigan December 1981.

The invitation secured me a B-2 Visa to Detroit, Michigan. I arrived in New York 1:15 pm 20 December 1981. I prayed on disembarking and I was grateful and thankful to God and Cloyd Ramsey having set foot once more on US soil. I thank Cloyd ceaselessly in my heart for having helped me escape to America despite the ignominy of being in exile and to seek asylum soon.

I caught my flight to Detroit, Michigan around 3:45 pm same day. The Ramsey's were at the Detroit Metropolitan International arrivals terminal waiting to receive me. They must have noted the fatigue in my face, if not the sorrow of leaving my beloved Gambia and people behind for an indefinite time. They welcomed me graciously and we headed for Sandusky, a small village in Michigan. I therein and then became part of the Ramsey family. Life has it that when some of us were created the mould broke. Most give their time and money to their own families or to work that brings them some happiness and some money. Cloyd Ramsey is among a few who give themselves wholly and unselfishly to others.

I can never be able to repay or tell how devoted Ramsey is in sharing life with the needy unless you meet him. In brief, Mr. Ramsey and wife Narrate fed and sheltered me when I needed food and place to stay until I get my feet back on earth.

He was my salvation voice in the wilderness of life's rugged road. I stayed as their guest in Sandusky until it was time to seek asylum at the Immigration and Nationality Service (INS) in Detroit.

There was no other situation less tense and so empty of hope than this next phase in my life. Life became an abyss of despair which only God and good friends, like the Ramsey's, pulled me out from underneath. Shakespeare said, between the acting of a dreadful thing and the first motion, all the interim is like a fantasy, or a hideous dream.

The genius and mortals instruments like to a little kingdom, suffers then the nature of an insurrection. Indeed an insurrection has been going on in my head during those horrible days of the coup d'état of April 15th 1980 I became aware of the need to muster courage, strength and endurance to prepare myself for the coming exile days and form it may take. Again,

Mr. Ramsey contacted the Gambia several time to no avail to verify and correct a possible misunderstanding that may have occurred. Several friends and legislators Ramsey contacted advised that I seek asylum from the INS. Senator Carl Levin sent us a package of three copies of Form 1-589 for my use on 6th January 1982.

We took the bull by the horns, completed the forms and Ramsey and I proceeded to INS office at Mount Elliot Street, Detroit, Michigan on the 22nd February 1982, were I was subsequently interviewed separately and told action will be rendered in four months earliest.

If wishes were horses beggars would gallop to heaven for it took well more than eight months before any reply came and only after numerous INS court hearings did we get some semblance of partial positive direction. The final act was left with the State Department and vice president's office.

Things were so delayed and difficult that I asked Ramsey to take me to the Catholic Mission for me to seek Sanctuary or more public help and support. We landed at St. Paul's Cathedral, Diocese of Michigan, where Hugh Davis led me to the refugee office of the Diocese.

On hearing my story the refugee co-coordinator, Mrs. Patricia Koblinsky called rev. Hugh C. White, advisor to the reigning Bishop of the Diocese, Bishop Coleman McGhee Jr. The Diocese received and let me stay at 44 Ledyard Street in Detroit. In the mean time Ramsey sent the following appeal to the INS office at Mount Elliot in Detroit, Michigan:

To whom it may concern

This letter is to acknowledge my association with Alhasan Ceesay, over a period of fifteen years. During that time I have found him to be a young man of very high ideals. His only interest in life has been to obtain an education and return to serve his home country and help his people.

I have personally invested thousands of dollars in Alhasan Ceesay because it seemed to me to be a very efficient way to help the impoverished people from his country that has had a great deal less than I have.

If anyone were to follow the course of his life, he would see that his motives most certainly were not to simply escape the futility of his home country and live that, good life here. There is no doubt in my mind that the dangers that he describes do exist for him.

Even if these were less than perfect proof, would you like to take the chance of being wrong and find out that he had been imprison or worse killed for no reason at all? Please save this man. If you cannot do it for his sake, then consider the investment made by concerned individuals, other organizations and myself.

Thank you for your serious considerations of this matter.
Signed: Cloyd Ramsey, Sandusky, Michigan

My next Alpena Samaritan and brother in Chris as well as profession was Dr. Charles T. Egli, who I met almost about the same time I did with Ramsey. He was a Surgeon working for the Medical Arts Clinic at the time of our meeting.

He came into the radar after a speech I gave to the Alpena Medical Association. He too has contributed prominently and was instrumental in having the medical Association comes to my aid with a donation of $400 towards my second semester fees at Alpena Community College. By this miracle I was able to complete payment for the second semester at college. Charles, as he prefers being called, is a surgeon and devoted Christian who also became very close friend and had done a lot to encourage my efforts.

His rallying for assistance continued throughout his days at the Medical Arts Clinic. For you to note Dr. Egli's closeness here is a letter he sent in my behalf during my petitioning for asylum in the USA. It read:

Medical Arts Clinic
211 Long Rapid road
Alpena, Michigan, 49707
November 14, 1986

RE: Deportation Notice on Alhasan Ceesay
Dear Senator Levin,
Alhasan Ceeesay was a college student in Alpena many years ago when I first met him and was very much impressed by his sincerity and enthusiasm. He went onto graduate school at Michigan Technological University in Houghton, Michigan, in hopes of getting into medical school.

He tried very hard to get into medical school in Africa. He was receiving no support from his own country because it considered him a political agitator and tribalist.

Alhasan Ceesay on his own initiative was able to get into medical school in Monrovia Liberia and succeeded in taking two years medical education before he fled for safety to the USA. He later sought political asylum in the USA for fear of persecution due to the aftermath of an attempted coup in July 181. It has always been his desire to complete his medical training and return to the Gambia when the climate warrants.

For almost five years now, Alhasan has been trying to receive asylum, during which time his chances at medical school are affected. Most recently he received a letter from INS judge ordering his deportation.

The deportation of Alhasan Ceesay back to the Gambia would result in his certain death or imprisonment and would constitute another tragedy in the way our government handles people like Alhasan. In a country where there are so many illegal aliens it seems that there must be some place for one more refugee. I beg you to personally consider Alhasan's case.

Sincerely

Dr. Charles T. Egli, M. D.

Mr. Homer Shepard, resident of Flint Michigan, was also very kind to me while at Flint. He offered to lodge me during the summer of 1969 on securing a full time job at the St. Joseph Hospital on Flint, Michigan as nurse assistant.

Homer and wife offered to help defray rent expenses, which were taking a quarter of my earnings. With this help I was able to return to Alpena Community College at the end of the summer and pay my dorm and food bills and still had some pocket money to buy pens and other sundries during the semester. God blesses his heart. We lost contact since my return to Africa.

All letters to his address were redirected, as addressee no longer leaves here. Bishop Coleman Mcgehee had already blessed efforts of the hastily formed the CEESAY COMMITTEE. It became the adhoc committee and my Pegasus wing. Like any normal human gatherings we had our different ideas as to how to approach the asylum problem but all of it steered towards or sought better ways to meet the challenges and enigma about to end all that I stood for and worked hard for in life.

The brain storming sessions were very pragmatic if not practical and well-intended discussions. One of the exploratory searches for solutions led us to Mayor Harvey Sloan of Louisville, Kentucky. I met Mayor Sloan in 1976 when I was trying to get into medical school at the University of Louisville. Also we used to write each other while I was in Monrovia, Liberia, West Africa.

I was invited to his office early February 1983, and was given opportunity to talk with key aids at the Louisville City Hall while he attended other state affairs. His executive aids, Sharon Wilbert and Mrs. Blanche reviewed my case along with information already in my file open in my name. They concluded that I did deserve help and I was asked to speak to Mrs. Joyce.

JoceJ. Rayzer, Director, and Health Affairs for the Mayor. Joyce contacted the Dean of the Medical School and gave him an in-depth briefing of my background and precarious situation I was faced with. Two weeks later on February 28th 1983, I received the following letter from Joyce in behalf of Mayor Harvey Sloan.
It read thus:

Office of the Director of Safety
City Hall
Louisville, Kentucky 40202
28 February 1983

Dear Mr. Ceesay,

It appears, as the old saying goes, that I have good news and bad news. I have been in contact with the University Of Louisville School Of Medicine with regards to your admission at the fall term. I have spoken to Dr. Donald Kemetz, Dean of the Medical School, and Mr. Harold Adams, Special Assistance to the president of the University of Louisville.
Both of these administrators upon reviewing the information you sent me; feel that you are a very good candidate for the minority admission program. There is however, one issue, which must be resolved favorably before your admission to medical school, or the financing and packaging necessary to begging this endeavor can be given serious considerations.
The issue, which must be resolved, is the financial determination base on whether you would be granted asylum in the country. Without the asylum being granted and hence financial aid the university cannot proceed with your request for admission this fall because your legal status would be too tenuous for them to invest hard cash in your future medical development under such nebulous state.mIt appears that you must begin medical school anew.
The two years completed at Liberia, cannot be accepted for transfer. You will start as freshman upon being granted asylum in USA.

Again, try and find resolution to granting you asylum. I have been assured that everything that can be done for you will be done immediately upon a favorable notice of your asylum. Everybody in the Mayor's office says hello, and we are sending you our prayers.
Sincerely
Joyce J. Rayzer
Director, Health Affairs

This was the impact Mayor Harvey Sloan had. In addition Mayor Harvey Sloan sent the following directly from his desk to the INS pleasing for them to grant me asylum.

City Hall
Office of the Mayor
Louisville, KY 40202
November 7, 1983

Alhasan S. Ceesay of the Gambia has contacted this office in an effort to gain political asylum in other to complete his medical education at the University of Louisville. I know that he is dedicated individual and is more desirous of providing needed medical aid to his fellow man.

Mr. Ceesay petitioned for political asylum in February 22, 1982 due to a purge, which followed a failed coup in the Gambia.The Medical school at the university of Louisville is currently processing his application for the 1984/85 academic years. It would be most helpful if you could assist him in expediting his papers. He will not be admitted unless a written statement confirming his residency status is available.

Since he has already lost two years awaiting residency confirmation, it would be deeply appreciated if you could assist this young man in any way possible. If my staff or I can be any further assistance in the matter, please do not hesitate to contact this office.

Sincerely
Harvey L Sloan
Mayor Louisville

Let us for a moment revert to Bishop Coleman McGhee at the Episcopal Diocese of Michigan in Detroit Michigan. Below is letter sent to the INS director, Edwin Chauvin at Mount Elliot in Detroit Michigan.

Dr. Alhasan Sisawo Ceesay, MD
Office of the Bishop
4800 Woodward Avenue
Detroit, Michigan 48201
24 October 1983

Dear Mr. Chauvin,

As Bishop for the Episcopal diocese of Michigan, located in Detroit, Michigan, I write you this letter on behalf of Alhasan S. Ceesay, a petitioner for political asylum in the United States.
As you may note from the file Mr. Ceesay seeks political asylum base on his fear of political persecution and danger to his physical safety and well being by the government, were he to be returned by the INS to his country the Gambia.

Mr. Ceesay's life will disclose to you, he was active opponent of the political regime in the Gambia.

After protesting incarceration of his friends, Mr. Ceesay was placed on a list of individuals who were allegedly involved in criminal activity and who were involved with the Movement for Justice in Africa (MOJA) and were sought for interrogation by the Gambia government.

The Gambia government has singled our Mr. Ceesay because of his political opposition and has prevented him from continuing his medical education in Liberia by cutting off his financial assistance and by asking the Liberian government to return Mr. Ceesay to the Gambia. I am personally acquainted with Mr. Ceesay, and believe him to be an individual who is worthy of support of the Episcopal Dioceses of Michigan.

I feel that it took great courage for Mr. Ceesay to stand up for human rights and to publicly oppose the political regime in the Gambia. I am convinced that Mr. Ceesay is an altruistic individual who deserves to pursue his medical training to benefit, both in the United States and perhaps elsewhere, those individuals who might be helped by his medical ability. Mr. Ceesay has already establish his medical science aptitude in his studies at Medical School in Liberia, and he has applied to and been accepted by the School of Medicine at the University of Louisville, Kentucky, with tuition to be paid by that institution, upon his authorization to remain in the United States.

Mr. Ceesay has also sought authorization to engage in employment pending the outcome of his asylum request, he proposes to assist in medical research at the university should his employment authorization be granted by your office.

Therefore, on behalf of Mr. Ceesay as well as the members of my Diocese, I would urge you to give favorable consideration to Mr. Ceesay's petition and expedite his request for employment and his political asylum petition in every possible way so that his efforts to enter the University of Louisville School of Medicine may not be delayed any longer than may be necessary by legal and administrative procedures which you office follows. Please feel free to contact me if I can be of any assistance in helping you to reach your determination on this matter. I fervently believed that, upon your investigation of Mr. Ceesay's case, you would reach the conclusions that he would be an asset to the United States, and that his fears as to his persecution and personal safety should he return to the Gambia, have firm foundation in fact.

Very truly yours
(The Rt. Rev.) H. Coleman McGhee, Jr.
Bishop of Michigan

The Bishop of Michigan, H. Coleman McGhee followed the above with a letter to then vice president George Bush Sr. Who sent the following tars reply.

The Vice President
Washington, D. C
April 25, 1984

Dear Rev. McGhee,

Thank you for your recent letter concerning Alhasan S. Ceesay. It was thoughtful of you to write and I appreciate your having taken the time to bring Mr. Ceesay's case to my attention. I have asked the State Department to review all asylum cases and human rights violations, which are brought to my attention.

I have, therefore shared your letter and the enclosures with officials at the Department of State and asked that they review Mr. Ceesay's request and write to you directly. I have also asked that a copy of their response be forwarded to my office. With best wishes
Sincerely
George Bush

Bishop McGhee, Bishop Mason, Rev. Hugh C. white, Rev. David Brower, Rev. Bill Woods, Rev. Virgil Jones, and Rev. Mark D. Meyer all touched my heart in similar fashions Hence here is my collective feeling and experience in a nut shell about these devoted men of Christ.

All of the priests lived in Detroit, Michigan except Rev. Mark D. Meyer, who lived in Plain view, Texas, USA. I lived with Rev. Mark Meyer in 1989 after hurricane Hugo devastated our campus at Montserrat, West Indies. The rest of the above I met while trying to defray deportation notice from the INS.

Those were challenging and nerving political moments for m family and I. These men of God never docked when told about my nightmare. These true believers became unique brothers I would like to share few outstanding things they did in style engraved in simple devotion to Christ's dictum.

I write because these men impressed me in their interpretations and devotion to the Gospel of Christ. Hence forgive me if I became a bit sentimental in relaying help they gave to me at various challenging times of my life. They were personal pastors for me.

These were the beacon of hope and faith that stood by me when it was all doom and gloomy for me. They were simple people, humble ones at that, I can confide with, debate with, and had shoulders on which to cry my heart out without being embarrassed and above all expect a little prayer at the end of it.

Then guess what? We would be on tract trying to get hold of friends of theirs and people that might lighten my burden. Their devotion to justice and fairness was magnanimous and are my brothers in Christ.Rev. Mark Meyer, on being told the hardship I endured in Montserrat from hurricane Hugo gave me a room and gifts more than ten thousand us dollars to help me complete my pre-clinics at the American University School of Medicine.

I learnt from these men of God that there is a special strength that can sustain us through almost any difficulty. That strength comes from God and from kind hearts like these Samaritans of good will. The strength comes from partly within but even more, it comes from faith and love of those close to us. These men gave themselves wholly and as unselfishly to others in need when I met them at the Episcopalian diocese of Michigan.

They devoted time to my cause and dropped selfish interests aside to help me fight my case against the INS while I was up to my neck in legal and political mud. I found nothing in these men but admirable integrity, honesty and unswerving commitment to leading life devoted to God, the Bible and in helping the downtrodden. I always feel elated whenever I get chance to speak to these kind hearts from afar. Meeting them makes me feel reunited with my best friends. I rather have a million more like then than multimillionaires that do not care about the plight of the common man.

Again, I applaud contribution and friendship these men touched my heart and life with. God blesses them. My family, villagers and I are extremely indebted to them. These men translated their concerns, and love of humanity and continued to be my good Samaritans and a bridge over trouble waters.

These believe in the worthiness and sanctity of life. And above all they ascribe to the power of knowledge and justice over ignorance. We look forward to the day we can serenade them amongst us in the smiling coast of the Gambia.

We pray they keep fit to be able to join us in the opening ceremony of the Manding Medical Centre at Njawara village, the Gambia, West Africa. These men translated their deep faith, concerns, and love of humanity.I opted to do my clinical rotations in Colchester, Essex, UK in 1990 and chanced to meet the Robinson's. Keith Robinson vested my newly born baby girl,

Famatanding Ceesay, at the Colchester County Hospital, which marked our first meeting. This slightly shy bloke impressed me a lot. He was all smiles and fund. He titled the little ears of my daughter and told her not to be as bad as her daddy. We all laughed over it.We from that moment liked each other and he became one of my inseparable unique Brits.

Keith and wife would visit the Gambia and my girls loved them to bits. Not for the presents he takes to them each time but because of his amiable personality, altruistic, very caring human he is.

He had spent boxes of monetary aid towards my NGO, Manding Medical Centre at Njawara village, and the Gambia. On the forming of the Friends Manding Charitable Trust, he was unanimously voted chairman of the charity by the members.

He had since inspiration of the Friends of Manding Charitable Trust worn the cap admirably and did a job well done for the charity. Also he had been instrumental in the Gambibazaar held every fortnight in Colchester to help raise funds for Manding Medical Centre's goals back in the Gambia.

He is committed to seeing the center come to fruition for the villagers of the Gambia and any that would need its service. Personally, he and his wife had been my lifeline and support. They have always come to my aid the call of expectation and I remain profoundly grateful to him and his wife Lorna V. Robinson.

Ten years ago I was on the verge of preparing becoming a consultant and return to serve the Gambia. Today an untold anguish my life went through in these years was dampened by kindness of Lorna and Keith Robinson and many other kind and generous Brits.

They are my Colchester Samaritans and Njawara villager's angels with golden hearts. We are working hard to seeing that manding Medical center transcends the dream it was to reality for the Lower Badibou region. Its service is much needed by the villagers. God blesses their hearts.

In Manchester many helped but few match Neville Brown, Kofi Awudo and Ahmed Nizami. Neville and I first met in Montserrat, West Indies while I was a medical student at the American University of the Caribbean.

We have ever since been cordial and upon finding me out in Manchester he had steadfastly kept that friendship ablaze. He in various ways would come to my aid with small but significant donations at the time.

He even helped in securing a job at Belfry House Hotel at Hands Forth in 2006. He is kindhearted fellow and my Montserrat. Kofi Awudo is Toggles gentleman I also met through his link with Neville Brown.

He turned to be very kind and generous to me. He bought me shoes and shirts to allow me start work at the above hotel. Years later on my return from Glasgow, Scotland he was the one that lodged me free of charge for three winter months. He is of exceptional quality and humane person. I remain grateful both fellows.

I met Mr. Ahamed Nizami in 2008, an angel in human flesh, at waseem's work place in Manchester. This lawyer turned Editor and I gelled from that hour to today. He is currently the Chief Editor of the Khalish Magazine, an Urdu language magazine in UK and worldwide. He also doubles as one of the Pakistani group leader in Manchester.

On knowing my predicaments his benevolence surfaced. There nod then he promised to help me with some the problems pulling me down and also indicated interest in helping my NGO Manding Medical Centre get financial aid to get a head start on the provision of its goals for the villagers. In addition he proposed a fun raising idea using his medium and other avenues that may come to light.

We tentatively initiated, depending on approval and provisos set by Keith Robinson, Chairman of Friends of Manding Charitable Trust in Colchester been met, formation of the Manchester manding Medical Center Annex to be office at 9 knowley Street in Manchester. To further demonstrate his kindness and interest in my goal Ahmed Nizami donated fees for all three PLAB exams I took in 2009.

A few more gentle hearts like Ganem Hadied felt sorry that life became so unkind and rough ride for me. He said, "Ceesay, I wish I can help more to get you out of the limbo you found yourself. Just believe in God and this pain will one day pass like history."

Friends such as Lorna Robinson, Eliza Jones, Mahmud Adam, Ganem Hadied, Abdinnisir, Faisal, Yusuf Ali, Ishfaque Ahmed, Ahmed Nizami, and countless angels all suffered my pain and fell through way into my heart through compassion as I plied through financial inadequacies.

Mahmud Adam also marched Ganem's effort by collecting money from the Liverpool mosque. Both monies were used for my exam fees and for which kindness I remain eternally grateful to all donors. Mohamed Salam of Greenhey business in Manchester was another Good Samaritan that came to my aid when I was left to sleep in cold weather at Alexandra Park.

Upon contacting him he kindly offered me room in one of his flats in Manchester. He was very kind and generous towards me. We have many times prayed together for my eventual breaking out of nightmarish bad luck life had been to me in recent times. Last but not the least is Sami Bati from Algeria who I stayed with at 245 Great Western

Street and who relentlessly called and ask people and friends to come to aid. He raised a bundle to help me pay school fees for my daughters in the Gambia and feed my bones. My friend and Brother Abdoullah Hashim and wife Asiya Qadri were very kind Bangladesh cum Pakistani couple I met during the most challenging times of my life. Their kindness is yet to be matched by their peers.

I met the couple while sleeping rough in the street of Manchester as Mohamed Salam' offer of a place came to an abrupt end.

The place was rented to a family leaving me homeless with no place to go except spend the nights at cold and treacherous Alexandra Park. It was very risky but being jobless it was the only option left to me.

Hence, it was a miracle when this God fearing Good Samaritan couple came to my rescue. They not only lodged me temporally at their other flat at 2 Sway field in Manchester but also continued to shower me with gifts and food.

I certainly look forward to hosting and having my villagers and family serenade this unusually kind and generous couple from Bangladesh. Yankuba Suso and dear friend Abdinnisir, Faisal and Dr. Haidar Shali deserve a mention with gratitude and thanks for kindness and generosity they showered me with during these dark days and for constantly reminding me that I am more than capable of bringing my dream to fruition for the villagers. Another of my Samaritan angels was young a man from Somali,

Yusuf Ali. He was among those who made certain I had food and he always comfort me by assuring me that God's day would be more rewarding. He said, "That day all your pain will be erased instantly and will enjoy the embrace of your family." I look forward to him being my guest in the Gambia. Mrs. Roheyata Corr-Sey, a cousin, remained the most supportive and one that kept encouraging me more than any family member had done during this challenging sojourn of mine.

God blesses her and her family. I look forward to being able to thank her in person for insisting that blood is thicker than water and for being with me in thick and thin of this murderous trail. I just have to have continued faith; confidence to do it and the universe will cooperate to justify these days difficulty.

My life being as mythical as Pelebstine fever, it was full of ups and downs and again it was Ahamed Nizami who offered to lodge me when I was asked to leave my previous address where I was renting. His kindness is phenomenal and transience's mortals.

Each day became a specific thrill that lead to that exhilarating moment of victory for mankind. It was a hard challenge and a march placed before me. It is a march I will pursue towards the day I would once again be able to serve the Gambia as a physician.

Friends such as Lorna Robinson, Eliza Jones, Mahmud Adam, Ganem Hadied, Abdinnisir, Faisal, Yusuf Ali, Ishfaque Ahmed, Ahmed Nizami, and countless angels all suffered my pain and fell through way into my heart through compassion as I plied through financial inadequacies.

Angels like Faisal, Abdal Rhaseed, Abdinnisir, Yusuf Ali, and Mahmud Adam deserved to be classed as paragons of kindness. These Somalis are among many who refused to let me bit the dust because of foot dragging visa problem. They encouraged by sharing food and they had with me and made certain that I persevere for a bright day for family and country. These are people who help lift my feet when my wings could not remember how to fly away from hardship. Faisal would on week ends prepare hot and well spiced Spaghetti and meat, or buy food for me from the next door restraint.

Abdinnisir in almost tearful manner would push me into going to get food. On top of this generosity these folks let me stay in their flat at 284 Great Western Street, Manchester while my lawyer fight not only to untangle but to get the Home office act on change of status request I made to that office back in 2004.

I feel favored, if not blessed having to face these inhuman challenges without losing my sanity. Being in the belly of a ferocious beast is more comfortable than life I am currently saddled. I feel like being at the interface between Purgatory and hell on earth. Simply put it is no domain for the weak for dilemma in this life remain ceaselessly changing.

This band of altruistic brothers kept me going through many a dark hour of my life in America and Great Britain. They stood tall for me among many in caring for the plight of those who they never met in poverty stricken parts of the world.

In this almost inhospitable life friends like these are a great gift indeed. Tinged with trepidations for what the future can sing I picked up courage and inspiration knowing that good comes out of fighting for what one believes in.

Life has taught me how to look after myself and that things do not just happen, people make it happen.

And so the villagers and I appeal for your help and participation with Manding Medical Centre.

Together we can walk on water and make this dream of providing medical aid to villages become worthy cause for generations. I have learnt not to rest on my oars else I fall into a deep and turbulent sea of troubles. I have to keep running in order to be with the best or where I am.
I will continue to not only learn to improve my performance but to work hard to see that this dream of providing a much needed medical aid to villagers is brought to fruition.

Dalliance said, say of me what you will and the morrow will judge you, and your words shall be a witness before its judgment and a testimony before its justice. I came to say a word and I shall utter it. Should death take me ere I give voice the morrow shall utter it. That which alone I do today shall be proclaimed before the people in the days to come.

Alasan Mballow, Son-Inlaw, 2014

I Rest My Case

Paul in a letter to Timothy 2 said, "I have fought a good fight, I have finished my course, and I have kept the faith." I hand this work for you to be judge of the ravages of the years and how my life was that of extreme ups and downs. In reality, I am very grateful to God even though my life met with various misfortunes, the most unbearable being the delay in my becoming a physician.

My life as witnessed in my books was an assembly of trials and tribulation emanating from roadblocks placed on my path by inhuman laws and unfortunate dark circumstances. Life has taught me to submit to divine decrees, whatever they may be from God.

It has in addition also taught me that if I want something done it was I who most do it and not expect anyone to hand golden Plata to me for it. For me helping others gives me great buzz.

I feel on the whole overly rewarded and delivered even though I had no family here in England nor was I as lucky as others who can feel and experience the warmth of their wives and children on daily basis. I succumbed to it as the way things were going to be for me and lived with this state of lonely affairs while in Manchester, England.

I experienced various turns of fate, enough for ten elephant loads, while on the little moat of the silver sea called England.

With my travels I was able to see Europe, the Americas and have learnt a great deal from it and met very kind people as well as experienced numerous unforeseen adventures thrown on my path. My life in England was full of pain; fear of deportation, hunger, extreme poverty due to joblessness, solitude and missing my wife and children I loved dearly.

I had a huge sense of duty in relation to the villagers and was not ready to fail them because of personal comfort or pleasures. Consequently Manding Medical Centre and benefits to be accrued from it and my family became my most if not the only occupation and direction in life.

Here is Manding Medical Centre if managed well it will do justice to rural health service for the next generation of Gambians to build upon.

Let me assure readers I never for one moment allowed ambition to get Manding Medical going blanketed my commitment to my family. I sent them every penny I laid hands on to the point of starving myself by having semolina and sardines as permanent diet.

The medical center is now a recognized charity in both the United Kingdom and America. I am committed to serve the villagers so that life of the children and young people would be better than mine when I was young.

I hope Manding Medical Centre becomes a model testimony of the boy from Njawara village who doggedly struggled to become a doctor and despite various twists of life is able to provide medical aid and service to villagers in rural Gambia. May be this will strengthen some other fellow to strive to do better than I did to bring health and happiness to the region. I hope my adventure persuades youngsters that man is capable of a lot more than he thinks he is capable of.

Our footprints must be inspirational to give heart to new coming Gambian generations.

Twenty years ago none would dream of thinking me becoming an author or to challenge powers as I did in this little frame and life of mine. I met a beautiful Maraka girl while I was in Monrovia, Liberia, West Africa. Fatou Koma is younger daughter of Elhaj Ansuman Koma and Jalian Ture of Kindia, Guinea Conakry, West Africa.

Her positive attitudes towards me lead our meeting on weekends at Cousin Sainabou Jobe's home. We started going out together and very soon I had the courage to ask her hand in marriage. There was no bone of contention with regards for my love for her. She was the darling of my heart at first sight and I was not going to let a fly land on her from that day onwards.

We had a simple wedding because her father did not quite approve of me because of fear for his uneducated but very pretty daughter being dump at one stage of the marriage for another educated city girl. I, in the long run, allied his fears and he ended up being one of my best friends and confidants I had up to the day he went to his maker.

Fatou Koma-Ceesay and I are blessed with three beautiful daughters, princesses Famatanding Ceesay, Binta Ceesay and Roheyata Ceesay. All of who, unlike me, had their schooling start at the age of five. The elder girl is aspiring to become a doctor and had been admitted to start her premed courses at Alpena Community College in Alpena, Michigan, USA.

Together Fatou Koma-Ceesay, the children and I went through all the tragedy of hunger, poverty and other sad experiences my sojourn in the quest of the Golden flees for the villager brought to us.

Fatou Koma-Ceesay initially hated Manding Medical Centre for she felt it consumed me and took me away from her and the children. The call got me entangled in a web of unfortunate circumstances and laws. The marriage had at one point almost spiraled to its end as wife' move became questionable. Nonetheless she remained a good mother and wife who took care of the girls in my absence.

My mother in-law was battered by confusion and as to why Fatou stuck it out with me under such immense hardship. Love is stronger glue! We loved each other and so we were able to stand by the other in good or bad times and my trip to England was the worse ever in our connubial life.It caused great turbulences in the marriage but I stuck with it for love's shake and the children who I love dearly.

Today, we are back together as family under the same roof while planning and supporting future of our darling girls. God bless Fatou Koma-Ceesay's heart and be reassured of endless love I have for her.For now Dalliance said it best for me when he said, "Say of me what you will and the morrow will judge you, and your words shall be a witness before its judgment and a testimony before it justice.

I came to say a word and I shall utter it. Should death take me ere I give voice; the morrow shall utter it. That which alone I do today shall be proclaimed before the people in days to come." I wrote with the hope the life enshrined herein will serve not only as an inspiration to the despondent but a lesson never to allow this sort of experience it passed through this planet.

I wrote in the hope that life enshrined in my books will serve not only as an inspiration to the despondent and downtrodden but a lesson never to allow this sort of experience it passed through this planet. I wrote because I felt that my life has something worth revealing to the world to engender tolerance and understanding between people and their governments.

I risked revealing today for all of us to learn from it and move to a better and rewarding future. Among the forces of life is one that stands a certain lofty peak a few is endowed with or able to explore its heights.

Ambition urges us to leave the lower surface of earth where the ordinary people live and ascend to heights that pierce the heavens. This mission has led to numerous Erie paths but for me this Pell-mell towards a better medical service for the neglected villager was a worthwhile adventure.

I am profoundly grateful and indebted to my wife Fatou Koma-Ceesay and our daughters, princesses Famatanding Ceesay, Binta Ceesay and Roheyata Ceesay for enduring all the pains that we went through in thick and thin times during my sojourn to America and England.

Also my deepest gratitude goes to Cousin Yata Sey-Corr for helping keep my family hopeful. God bless her heart eternally. I forgive my own brothers and sisters who refused to cater for my family in my absence. Hello, hats off to Sey Kunda.

Cousin Rohey Yata Sey with grand son, Banjul, Gambia

THE WAY OF A DREAMER

Back in the Gambia a friend decried my efforts as nothing but a dream that I persistently chased. I let such observers know that it only takes time before my dream become fruitful. Here are a few examples: I left the Gambia in 1967 as a nurse and returned; after insurmountable roadblocks as a medical doctor.

While practicing in the Gambia I further created two worthy entities, namely (1) The Gambia Health Credit Union, which today provides needed financial assistance to all health workers i.e. Nurses and Health Inspectors country wide. (2) In addition I created NGO Manding Medical Centre at Njawara village, Lower Badibou to help provide a much needed medical aid and service free of charge to villagers who could not afford to pay private clinics.

With the help of visiting doctors the centre has treated more than 9000 villagers free of charge since its inception in 1993. On returning to the UK, I again with help of resident nurses and doctors in Colchester Essex setup the Friends of Manding Charitable trust in Colchester UK. This was recognized and registered as a charity in England and Wales by the UK- charity Commission in 2002.

 In the midst of which I published my first book 'The Legend Against all Odds' and now has published more than thirty eight novels. To further cement my goal for the villager I was able to convince the Alpena City Council to form a sister city link with Njawara and Kinte Kunda villages in the Lower Badibous of the Gambia in 2005.

This was made easier after my being awarded on May 5th, 2005 'Distinguished Graduate Award' by Alpena Community College.

My web site: friends of Manding gambimed continues to lure people to Njawara to see what help they could give the villager. Today, I am not only an author of several books; Google search: Dr. Alhasan Ceesay/books to view of purchase as contribution to rural healthcare; portions or sales from these books go to support goals of Manding medical Centre at Njawara. I am indeed a dreamer and will continue to dream fir my people.

If the above is dream then here is another step to help see through me. I am humble to let you know I am now a Publisher and my company in the UK is 'PUBLISH KUNSA LTD' and one can have their work published by logging on to our web site; www.publishkunsa.com. Again two pounds sterling from any book published by my company goes towards scholarships and rural healthcare as stipulated in terms of contract we would work on manuscripts.

Dreams must be activated and not wasted. I cannot fly without wing but can make artificial wings to let reach higher hits that loafers never can dream of. Allow the dream to force you into action. Yes, I too have a dream, which is simply that every hamlet in the Gambia be bequeathed good healthcare, safe drinking water, enough food and chance to a solid education for every child.

Yes. Education is power and a mover. I sacrificed my life to endure depravity, humiliation and solitude in other to bring medical aid to villagers. With all these I am busy trying to get more medical skills and experience before heading to Gambia, home , sweet home. With this tit-bit I can freely and willingly encourage you to dream but not to let it remain at that.

A life with trials or challenge is like an orchestra without conductor and it very defeating if not boring indeed. One must act for the good of self and any community we find ourselves. An old village sage once advice that 'A good person and at best a leader never yield to failure but only learns from it to move forward.

Grand Pa Bajoja Ceesay told me that; "One willing to do good should not expect people to remove obstacles or stones from their path; but such leaders must accept it calmly in the event these place more boulders on our way." This is what a dream turns out. At first it becomes a lonely avenue full of heartaches, which eases gradually as the good things unfold from one's relentless efforts to make the dream becomes fruitful and rewarding..

Simple its life 99.9% very hard work full of stumbling. Do not we all dream of going to heaven? Well the path to such respites need challenging theological and spiritual discipline. Hence we earthly dreamers dabble with ideas of landing on Mars and eventually colonizing it. So allow me ask, what is your dream for mankind, especially Africa? Can Africa ever be free of ignorance, self subtenant, corruption and misuse of the tribe? These just few multipronged toxic dragon heads African must dream to remove from our midst. With better education and discipline Africa can overcome and progress. Dreamers are doing utmost to slay the pestilent dragon hindering life in the villages of rural Africa.

We must remove the monster of retro ration for the shake of the future generation. Again grandpa Bajoja Ceesay advices that we stay the good cause and never be taken by detractions. I am no millionaire but have a million dreams worthy of pursuing for my people.

Would you dream along with me? Glad to let you know hard work yields rewarding fruits. Dream and be in control of not only your own life but be a source of hope and inspiration while contributing positively to your community. Do not be carried along by current get rich quick and live selfishly. Life is to be shared even with dreamers.

Time is not mine and life will continue for the villager. Success comes slowly and brings with it contagious hope that serves as blue print for other. The fate of mankind is up to each of us. Do not succumb to idleness. Use youthful opportunity to develop out of ignorance, and corruption by having courage to bring change to the people.

Be the change you want in others. Expect resistance on your path to bring change. A useful proxy in fulfilling a dream is not letting it wane away. Always think it possible and work hard at its realization. Be warned to think what could be done and not that which cannot be archived. Matrix of success lies in hard work with guided ski full knowledge.

I will work on my dream and morrow will be my judge along with benefits accrued from it. I hope my last footprints of my journey on earth will inspire people towards doing well and sharing their worth with others. From one villager to another may this wish be true for rural Gambia.

Dr. Alhasan Ceesay holding Africa

ABOUT THE AUTHOR

I was born in 1946 at Njawara Village, Lower Badibou District in the North Bank of the Gambia. I am a scion of a Mandinka and Fulani tribe and am one of five siblings.

I had my education at Kinte Kunda, then Armitage High School, ending up as a registered nurse at the Royal Victoria Hospital, Banjul, before embarking to the USA on my medical degree quest.

I graduated from the American University School of Medicine in Montserrat, West Indies, in 1992 and returned to the Gambia to start setting up a self-help village health NGO Manding Medical Centre.

The Gambia Government and the Badibou local authority registered NGO Manding Medical Centre in 1993. The centre has treated and provided medicines to more than 9000 patients free of charge.

I am married to Fatou Koma-Ceesay and we are blessed with three beautiful girls, Famatanding Ceesay, Binta Ceesay and Roheyata Ceesay. Unlike me, all of them started school early without the roadblocks I had to cross in my early years.

I am currently a medical officer at the Royal at the Royal Victoria Hospital on study leave. It is my hope that this work will inspire others and bring much needy help to providing medical service to rural Gambia.

Dr. Alhasan Ceesay displays first book published 2002

Mission

Our objective is to improve the healthcare delivery to villagers, educating youths on STD and Drugs and quality of life for the people in rural Gambia. The Manding Medical Centre strives to accomplish this goal through primary health care and disease prevention, the promotion of health policy, health research and increased access to health care education for the people in the Gambia.

Have your manuscript become a book by submitting it for possible publication to acquisitions publishes Kunsa. Com

Please contact us to expose your work globally.

PUBLISH KUNSA.COM

GAMBIA HAS DECIDED TO BE FREE: PRESIDENT ADAMA BARO WHEELNG YAHYA JAMMEH TO EXILE IN GUINEA EQUITORIAL JANUARY 2017

www.ingramcontent.com/pod-product-compliance
Lightning Source LLC
Chambersburg PA
CBHW071147160426
43196CB00011B/2037